GEORGE WASHINGTON
AS THE FRENCH KNEW HIM

Le Général a constamment dans la bouche le principe que la qualité de Citoyen est la première et celle d'officier la Seconde—GÉRARD.

GEORGE WASHINGTON
AS THE FRENCH KNEW HIM

A COLLECTION OF TEXTS

Edited and Translated, with an Introduction by

GILBERT CHINARD

GREENWOOD PRESS, PUBLISHERS
NEW YORK

Contents

Illustrations

The motif on the title page was taken from the title page of
Montesquieu, *De l'Esprit des Loix*. Nouvelle édition.
Amsterdam, 1749. The motto EX RECTO DECUS seemed to
sum up excellently the opinions of Washington's French
contemporaries and historians, and for this reason is here
reproduced.

WASHINGTON   *frontispiece*

Drawn by Marckt, engraved by Bertonnier. From Chateaubriand, *Voyage en Amérique*. Œuvres complètes,
Paris, 1836. Vol. XII, p. 20.

WASHINGTON   *facing* 88

Engraved from the cameo made by Madame de Bréhan at
Mount Vernon, in 1789. From the frontispiece to the sec-
ond volume of St. John de Crèvecœur, *Voyage dans la
Haute Pensylvanie*. Paris, 1801.

PHYSIOGNOMIES   115

"Physiognomies of a few characters who played a part in
the French and American Revolutions." From J. M. Plane,
*Physiologie ou l'Art de connaitre les hommes sur leurs
physionomies*. Meudon, l'an 1797 (V.S.). Plate H, p. 329.

Introduction

While Benjamin Franklin has repeatedly attracted the attention of French historians, and Jefferson has not been entirely neglected, thanks mainly to his famous saying, more or less correctly reported, "Everyman has two countries . . . ," it would seem that, at least during the last hundred years, Washington has not aroused the same interest on the part of the French public. To the French of our time, he appears as a remote figure, known particularly because of his friendship for Lafayette, a somewhat distant hero whose unpronounceable name is the despair of the Parisian taxi-drivers. Who could blame the French for this ignorance when the Americans themselves repeat with McMaster, "George Washington is an unknown man"; with Channing, "As to the inner man we are strangely ignorant. No more elusive personality exists in history"; when John Corbin entitles the first chapter of his penetrating study on *The Unknown Washington*, "An air-hole in history"?

It cannot be said that the mystery has been dispelled by more recent studies, by the exact and painstaking biography of John Fitzpatrick, or the more impressionistic work of Mr. Bernard Faÿ, nor by the lengthy narrative of Mr. Rupert Hughes. In spite of the efforts of "debunking" historians, the first President remains surrounded with a sort of halo, he has become a national myth, the prototype of the strong silent man.

The series of impressions and notes reproduced here was not assembled with the ambition of correcting the views of Washington's biographers; it aims even less at presenting a full length portrait of the American hero. It happened, however, that a certain number of Frenchmen, volunteers serving under him, officers in Rochambeau's army, travelers and investigators had the opportunity to meet Washington, to sit at his table, to talk with him, or to try to make him talk; they watched him with intense curiosity and interest, they noted their impressions of the great man and sometimes made keener observations than any of the American contemporaries of George Washington have ever consigned in their diaries. Several of them were not entirely disinterested observers, but their notations are well worth preserving and studying.

The foundation for this collection was laid up, in fact, some twenty years ago by the late Ambassador Jusserand, in his book entitled *With Americans of past and present days,* New York, 1916. Almost ten years later, Professor Bernard Faÿ, in his work on *L'Esprit révolutionnaire en France et aux Etats-Unis,* Paris, 1925, mentioned incidentally Washington throughout his book and discussed more elaborately his popularity in France on the occasion of Fontanes' funeral oration. The scope of their studies prevented both authors from quoting extensively from their sources. Several of the works they mentioned have never been reprinted and are not easily obtainable, others have never been translated into English and for these reasons, perhaps, have been practically ignored by most historians; it is safe to assume at any rate that they remain unknown to most of the American devotees of Washington. No attempt has been made to compile a complete collection and deliberately two or three authors have been left out for reasons indicated later.

The classification adopted is natural and as far as possible chronological: the Frenchmen who served under Washington come first; the officers in Rochambeau's army follow; the travelers, diplomats and investigators of the time form a third group; the account of the ceremonies ordered by Bonaparte on the occasion of the death of Washington have been thought important enough to constitute a section; in a last group have been placed French authors who had not met Washington personally, but who were close enough to his time to echo the impressions of his contemporaries, the latest in date being

Tocqueville who could not be overlooked and Guizot whose study published in English exactly a hundred years ago was for a long time considered in France as the outstanding and authoritative work on Washington.

To discuss and evaluate these opinions would take a long time and much space. It seemed better to let the texts speak for themselves. It may not be amiss, however, to indicate briefly the main traits of Washington's character as seen by men whose admiration, unbounded as it was, was not colored by any national pride in the deeds of the American President. Long before the embellishments due to the fertile mind of Reverend Locke Weems, Washington appeared, at least to the French, as one of the greatest figures in the history of the world. Shortly after his death, Bonaparte, then First Consul, ordered that his statue be placed "in the Great gallery of the Tuileries," with those "de Démosthènes, d'Alexandre, d'Annibal, de Scipion, de Brutus, de Cicéron, de Caton, de César, de Gustave-Adolphe, de Turenne, du Grand Condé, de Duguai-Trouin, de Malborough, du prince Eugène, du maréchal de Saxe, du Grand Frédéric, de Mirabeau, de Dugommier, de Dampierre, de Marceau et de Joubert." (*Moniteur* Pluviose, 20, 1800.)

This extraordinary tribute paid by the victorious First Consul to the American soldier may seem astonishing to the modern historians who deny that Washington had any military talent. However great or small his genius as a tactician may have been, it was unanimously acknowledged by all the French volunteers who served on his staff, and more significantly by all the French officers who fought in Rochambeau's army. It is at least worthy of note to remember that these young men and these experienced soldiers who had met in the field Frederic's soldiers or studied his tactics in the Ecole Militaire, admired without any reservation the way Washington had planned and conducted the operations of his army before Boston, at Trenton, at Monmouth and Princeton. Not being a military historian, the editor does not feel qualified to pass judgment on their verdict. It seems, however, that the opinion

ix

of Alexandre Berthier, later and for almost fifteen years, chief of staff of Napoleon should not be lightly dismissed.* The fact that these tactics had been formulated to a large extent by a French volunteer, brigadier general Duportail, later Minister of War under the Revolution, does not lessen in any way the credit due to the man who put them into practice and persistently adhered to them.

Recognized as a military genius of the first order, Washington appeared to the French, even before the Revolution, as the embodiment of the citizen-soldier, and the great organizer of an army of citizens. The French officers were familiar only with professional armies, and without exception were themselves professional soldiers. They were filled with wonder at the sight of an army of farmers and workmen, led by men who only recently "had never handled a gun," but were practicing law or medicine or simply tilling their lands. Their supreme commander was a man whose previous experience had been practically negligible and somewhat unfortunate. The soldiers were badly clad if well fed, they were poorly armed; they had no sense of hierarchy, no great respect for rank since they elected their officers themselves, no military tradition, and yet Washington had succeeded in introducing order, discipline, sense of subordination and efficiency in what by all rights and precedents should have been an indescribable mob. To these somewhat sceptical professional soldiers, Washington succeeded in demonstrating beyond any doubt that a popular army could be made to fight and to win battles. Some ten years later more than one of these young officers and Rochambeau himself were to lead the French volunteers of 1792 who were marching "sans pain et sans souliers"; how could they help remembering at that time the "shoeless" soldiers of the battle of Trenton, staining the icy roads with the blood of their feet?

This was the example and the precedent mentioned by the orators of the French Revolution when the "patrie était en

* This point will be made clearer in a forthcoming edition of the Berthier papers, in the possession of Princeton University.

danger," and Brissot in a fiery speech made on July 10, 1791, before the Assemblée des Amis de la Constitution, urged the French volunteers to emulate their American predecessors:

O men, who doubt the prodigious and supernatural efforts that love of liberty can exact from men, consider what the Americans have done to conquer their independence. Look at Warren, a physician who had never handled a gun, defending the hillock of Bunkerhill, with a handful of Americans, badly equipped, badly trained, and before surrendering making more than twelve hundred English soldiers bite the dust of the battlefield. Follow the steps of General Washington resisting with 3 or 4,000 farmers more than 30,000 English soldiers and making game of them! Observe him at the battle of Trenton! He used to tell me that his soldiers had no shoes; that the ice which cut their feet was stained with their blood. *"To-morrow we shall have shoes,"* did they say, "we shall beat the English" . . . and beat them they did. (*Moniteur*, July 10, 1791.)

Two days later, the whole population of Paris attended the apotheosis of Voltaire, when the mortal remains of the philosopher were taken to the newly dedicated Temple des Grands Hommes. On the sarcophagus banked with "flowers from the fields" and oak leaves could be read two inscriptions:

> *Si l'homme est né libre, il doit se gouverner.*
> *Si l'homme a des tyrans, il doit les détrôner.*

In France where the fight for liberty had just begun, no man could be proposed to the nation as exemplifying the maxims of the champion of "Calas, la Barre and Montbailly"; but on the other side of the Ocean a man could be found who had fought against a tyrant and won liberty for his country. It was not a mere coincidence that on the two following days, July 13 and 14, the Théâtre de la Nation gave the first performances of a new tragedy in four acts *Vasington ou la Liberté du Nouveau Monde*. It had been announced for several weeks and was obviously a *pièce de circonstance*. The author M. de Sauvigny who had already praised the simple virtues of the American Indians in his tragedy *Hirza ou les Illinois* had turned this time to their worthy successors who, under the guidance of a Plutarchian hero had recently adopted a model constitution. Sauvigny was no great poet, but the play presents a real historical value. It will be studied elsewhere more in detail : a quotation from the final scene may be sufficient here to show that already, in the words of Brissot, the French Revolution considered itself as the direct offspring of the American Revolution and that, in the eyes of the friends of liberty, George Washington stood as the living exemplar of all the civic virtues :

VAZINGTON

A ce discours flatteur, à ces généreux traits,
Je reconnois le charme et le cœur d'un Français :
Heureux dans mes travaux d'avoir conquis l'estime
D'un peuple courageux, sensible et magnanime.
Que ce durable airain, aux siècles à venir,
De vos vaillans guerriers porte le souvenir,
Et dise qu'un traité, fruit de la bienfaisance,
Vient affermir les droits de notre indépendance.
J'ai donc vu sur la terre, enfin, l'égalité
Rendre à l'homme avili toute sa dignité,
Et, donnant à nos cœurs une force indomptable
Poser d'un vaste Etat la base inébranlable.

LAURENS

Idole de mon cœur, premier bien des mortels,
Liberté ! si mon sang arrosa tes autels,
Du moins, en terminant ma pénible carrière,
Tes bienfaisantes mains fermeront ma paupière.

It was already obvious that Washington had succeeded in saving his country in spite of the opposition he had met on the part of the mere politicians, in spite of the ill-will of Congress, in spite of the stay-at-home who complained that the war lasted too long. With a few exceptions he had held his men and his officers together, as a "faisceau"; he was more than a chief; he was a leader. Yet, by a strange contradiction, he was entirely devoid of personal magnetism: he inspired confidence more than enthusiasm, lasting respect more than passing admiration. Stranger even was the fact that he had no relish for military glory. His only ambition was to go back to his country house, which he used to call "my farm." As early as 1778, a much disappointed volunteer who liked neither men nor women in America, wrote a long poem, or rather a long lamentation which he sent to Paris and which was printed in the *Mémoires secrets pour servir à l'histoire de la République des Lettres*, under the date of November 17, 1779. In his universal detestation of all things American, he made one exception for Washington, standing like a giant among pygmies and already endowed with all the traits that tradition has attributed to him. Only the last stanzas are quoted here, from a manuscript found in Boston by the late Professor Van Roosebroeck.

Fait à Boston en 1778 par Mr. le Vicomte de Maurois, Lieutenant-Colonel

Maintenant mon cœur me seconde:
Je vais peindre un vrai citoyen,
Le Fabius du nouveau-monde,
Un héros, un homme de bien.

Il est d'une figure heureuse,
De beaux traits, de la dignité,
Sous une forme avantageuse
La plus noble simplicité.

Sensible, valeureux, fidèle,
Et révéré de l'ennemi,
L'honnête homme en fait son modèle,
Et l'homme aimable son ami.

xiii

Contre l'orage qui murmure,
Son courage en impose au sort,
C'est le calme d'une ame pure
Pour qui l'écueil même est un port.

J'ai vu Wassington sans armée,
Devant un ennemi vainqueur,
Et la cabale envenimée
Attaquer jusqu'à son honneur.

Du double coup qui le menace
Ce héros n'est point abattu,
L'Anglois respecte son audace,
L'envieux cède à sa vertu.

Il sait trop que pour entreprendre
L'art manque à ses braves enfans,
Ce qu'il n'oseroit en attendre,
La constance l'obtient du temps.

Jouet du fol, trésor du sage,
O temps qui nourris notre espoir,
Tu feras passer d'âge en âge,
Celui qui connoit ton pouvoir.

Ici la nature économe
N'irrite point les yeux jaloux :
Elle n'a produit qu'un grand homme,
Mais il est le salut de tous.

But this great citizen-soldier was also a great statesman
who had the ambition to give to the people he had saved the
most perfect form of government. He had no more taste for
power than for military glory, and yet he accepted the re-
sponsibilities placed upon him by his fellow-citizens, ready
to step out at any time when his work was done. He was
much more than a reincarnation of Cincinnatus going back
to his plough; he was an all-time example to be placed before
the eyes of would-be military dictators. Thus, Fontanes, on

August 22, 1797, wrote an article entitled *Washington proposed as an example to the leaders of another republic*. It was the same Fontanes who, three years later, on February 8, 1800, by order and in the presence of Bonaparte, delivered a funeral oration in which he hailed Washington as a character rightly belonging to the most famous periods of antiquity, "a man who died in retirement, as a private individual, in his native land, from which he had accepted the highest honors after making it free with his own hands."

Unaware of his destiny, Bonaparte himself provided on that day the foundation for the famous parallel that Chateaubriand was to write twenty-six years later, contrasting for all times the destroying sword of the military conqueror with the lasting virtues of the republican hero. This was not an isolated example, for the same admiration was expressed by Hyde de Neuville, a royalist at heart, by Tocqueville who endorsed but reluctantly democracy at its best, and by Guizot, the liberal minister of Louis-Philippe. Thus George Washington even after his death succeeded in obtaining recognition from French Bonapartists, monarchists, former émigrés and liberals for the highest and purest republican virtues of which he appeared as the living embodiment.

In him also they admired the man and the staunch friend. The eighteenth century has exalted friendship, and this American, so cold and so distant, had an extraordinary gift for winning the friendship of his associates. Here again contemporary testimonies may help to check historical supercriticism. When all is said about Lafayette's vanity, ambition and "canine thirst" for fame, a fact remains, attested by many contemporaries, the constant, faithful, undying friendship and esteem of Washington for his "dear Marquis" and the sincerity and the depth of the feelings of the young French nobleman for the American hero. No mere schemer would have obtained such a recognition from a man who was a good judge of character. Without any ostentation or display of generosity Washington was also adjudged by the French a model of philanthropy. The *Moniteur* again on August 16,

1791, published a significant extract from a letter written from Charleston on May 10:

"General Washington, who is travelling through the Southern States, has recently visited our province. Since his arrival all business has been suspended. Crowds surround the first Magistrate of the Federative Republic, all look up to him as the saviour of the country, all respect him as the founder of our States and cherish him as a father who would come to see for himself if his children are happy. He appears among us without any display, with no escort except his virtues, with no retinue except a secretary and the enduring memory of his beautiful and glorious deeds."

No picture can be complete without some shadows; here they serve only to place the high lights in better relief. When the French Republic and the United States became estranged, the French envoys, and particularly citizens Genet and Adet, thought it their duty to deflate Washington's reputation and to join the opposition against the President. Their opinion of Washington was clearly dictated by a partisan spirit, which was in no way encouraged by their home government. Among the travelers, as far as I know, only one, Bayard, made a point to collect all the gossip then current in Baltimore in a special section of the second edition of his *Voyage dans l'intérieur des Etats-Unis . . . pendant l'été de 1791*, Paris, an VI. It is significant that in conclusion he had grudgingly to admit that: "A man who managed to withdraw honorably from public life while preserving the means to start over again on a new career entirely opposed to the first, may be an unprincipled being, he cannot be a man without talents."

In the relations of our annalists, however, Washington does not always appear with this heroic halo. Many of them knew him intimately, they sat at his table, visited him at Mount Vernon, were received in the unpretentious house in which he lived while in Philadelphia. The great man could unbend and occasionally smile if he never laughed; he was most attentive to his guests and received them with the most perfect politeness, yet without any stiffness or affectation. Moré de Pontgibaud, Chastellux, Brissot, Crèvecœur have drawn unforgettable pictures of Washington at Valley Forge, in Philadelphia or at Mount Vernon. There one will see Washington taking the helm and directing a boat through the ice floes, not across the Delaware, but across the Hudson, not to attack the enemy, but simply to take a guest home and spare him a difficult road. Not the least important of these pictures will be found in a letter written by chevalier de Ternant to his Minister, after coming back to America as plenipotentiary of the French Republic. Its perusal is particularly recommended to the historians who like to represent the American diplomats and statesmen as guileless and powerless children with whom the wily Europeans can play at will. Ternant had a few words to say on the subject and George Washington as well as Mr. Jefferson could hold their own and play their cards against any negotiator trained in the old school.

The following generation of French travelers and writers did not alter the essential traits of the portrait of Washington as it had been drawn by his immediate contemporaries. To Hyde de Neuville, he remained a national hero typifying excellently the country of his birth. Barbé-Marbois, who in his younger days had known Washington in Philadelphia, had negotiated the sale of Louisiana, and served Napoleon and Louis XVIII, judged late in life that, "Washington remains greater in the eyes of his fellow citizens than Alexander or Cæsar ever were for the Greeks and the Romans." Tocqueville, more interested in institutions than in men, unaware of the part played by Washington in the making of the Constitution, praised him mainly for "the admirable letter which he addressed to his fellow citizens and which may be looked upon as his political bequest to his country." It remained for an experienced statesman and an eloquent writer to draw the conclusion. This was done by François Guizot, whose study many times reprinted was published in America exactly a hundred years ago.

Here we may stop, but not without wondering what were the reasons, perhaps ill defined but deep and almost permanent, which brought about this unanimous admiration of the French for a foreign hero. The answer is probably to be found in the sentence inscribed by Joseph Fabre at the beginning of his *Washington, libérateur de l'Amérique,* printed in 1882, at a time when the Third Republic still uncertain of its stability looked toward the future with doubt and fear : "A la mémoire de Lazare Hoche, le soldat citoyen, qui aurait été notre Washington s'il avait vécu." None of the heads of government chosen or accepted by France since the Revolution could tally with this ideal and none was in sight who could measure up to Washington. In the tributes paid by the French to the American President, there is a sort of melancholy and regretful yearning for a great military leader devoid of political ambition, for a great ruler placing the interests of the country before his own fame, for a great statesman able to establish and to make secure this rare combination of order and liberty without which democracies cannot survive. In the days of trial and wrath through which France is passing and which are so similar to the Directory, her rulers might well profit by remembering the advice given by Fontanes in his *Exemple de Washington proposé aux chefs d'une autre république.*

GILBERT CHINARD

Princeton University
August 1940

NOTE—The editor takes particular pleasure in expressing his appreciation of the precious encouragement he has received from the society of THE AMERICAN FRIENDS OF LAFAYETTE, and particularly from Messrs. Louis Annin Ames, Howard R. Cruse, Stuart W. Jackson, Walter P. Gardner, Messmore Kendall, J. Bennett Nolan and Maurice Léon.

G. C.

I.

The French Volunteers

LAFAYETTE
DUPONCEAU
DUPORTAIL
GOUVION
COLONEL ARMAND
MORÉ DE PONTGIBAUD

Lafayette

No extracts can do justice to the subject, and Lafayette's admiration and deep affection for Washington run through the whole set of the Marquis' *Memoirs*. The letters here reprinted speak for themselves. The first one was written at the time of the Conway cabal. The second was written by Washington and is but one of the many in which Washington unbent and expressed his warm feelings for the young Marquis. The third one sent by Lafayette to Steuben is probably as full a portrait of Washington as can be found anywhere in the *Mémoirs*. The fourth one was written by Lafayette when leaving for France in 1781. The two letters, written in 1784, contain the last adieu of the two friends. They are reproduced from the *Memoirs, Correspondence and Manuscripts of General Lafayette. Published by his family*. London. Saunders and Otley. 1837.

TO GENERAL WASHINGTON.*
(ORIGINAL.)

Camp, 30th December, 1777.

MY DEAR GENERAL,—I went yesterday morning to headquarters with an intention of speaking to your excellency, but you were too busy, and I shall lay down in this letter what I wished to say.

* This letter was occasioned by the momentary success of an intrigue, known in American history under the name of Conway's cabal. Conway, who wished to oppose Gates to Washington, had written to the former a letter, in which he attacked the general-in-chief. An aide-de-camp of Lord Stirling gained knowledge of that letter, and communicated its contents to Washington, who entered immediately into an explanation with Conway, in consequence of which the latter sent in his resignation, and announced the intention of re-entering the

3

I don't need to tell you that I am sorry for all that has happened for some time past. It is a necessary dependence of my most tender and respectful friendship for you, which affection is as true and candid as the other sentiments of my heart, and much stronger than so new an acquaintance seems to admit; but another reason, to be concerned in the present circumstances, is my ardent and perhaps enthusiastic wishes for the happiness and liberty of this country. I see plainly that America can defend herself if proper measures are taken, and now I begin to fear lest she should be lost by herself and her own sons.

When I was in Europe I thought that here almost every man was a lover of liberty, and would rather die free than live a slave. You can conceive my astonishment when I saw that toryism was as openly professed as whiggism itself: however, at that time I believed that all good Americans were united together; that the confidence of congress in you was unbounded. Then I entertained the certitude that America would be independent in case she should not lose you. Take away, for an instant, that modest diffidence of yourself, (which, pardon my freedom, my dear General, is sometimes too great, and I wish you could know, as well as myself, what difference there is between you and any other man,) you would see very plainly that if you were lost for America, there is no body who could keep the army and the revolution for six months. There are open dissensions in congress, parties who hate one another as much as the common enemy; stupid men, who, without knowing a single word about war, undertake to judge you, to make ridiculous comparisons; they are infatuated with Gates, without thinking of the different cir-

service of France. The resignation was not accepted by congress, and Conway was, on the contrary, named inspector-general of the army, with the rank of major-general, and the formation of the war office in relation to the mercenary troops. We see, by a letter from General Washington, that M. de Lafayette was the only person to whom he shewed General Conway's letter, transmitted by Lord Stirling's aide-de-camp.—(Letter to Horatio Gates, of the 4th of January, 1778, written from Washington. V. 1st, Appendix No. 6.)

4

cumstances, and believe that attacking is the only thing necessary to conquer. Those ideas are entertained in their minds by some jealous men, and perhaps secret friends to the British Government, who want to push you in a moment of ill humour to some rash enterprise upon the lines, or against a much stronger army. I should not take the liberty of mentioning these particulars to you if I did not receive a letter about this matter, from a young good-natured gentleman at York, whom Conway has ruined by his cunning, bad advice, but who entertains the greatest respect for you.

I have been surprised at first, to see the few establishments of this board of war, to see the difference between northern and southern departments, to see resolves from congress about military operations; but the promotion of Conway is beyond all my expectations. I should be glad to have new major-generals, because, as I know, you take some interest in my happiness and reputation: it is, perhaps, an occasion for your excellency to give me more agreeable commands in some interesting instances. On the other hand, General Conway says he is entirely a man to be disposed of by me. He calls himself my soldier, and the reason of such behaviour to me is, that he wishes to be well spoken of at the French court, and his protector, the Marquis de Castries, is an intimate acquaintance of mine; but since the letter of Lord Stirling I inquired in his character. I found that he was an ambitious and dangerous man. He has done all in his power, by cunning manœuvres, to take off my confidence and affection for you. His desire was to engage me to leave this country. Now I see all the general officers of the army against congress; such disputes, if known by the enemy, would be attended with the worst consequences. I am very sorry whenever I perceive troubles raised among the defenders of the same cause, but my concern is much greater when I find officers coming from France, officers of some character in my country, to whom any fault of that kind may be imputed. The reason of my fondness for Conway was his being by all means a very brave and very good officer. However, that talent for manœuvres,

5

and which seems so extraordinary to congress, is not so very difficult a matter for any man of common sense who applies himself to it. I must pay to General Portail, and some French officers, who came to speak to me, the justice to say, that I found them as I could wish upon this occasion; for it has made a great noise among many in the army. I wish, indeed, those matters could be soon pacified. I wish your excellency could let them know how necessary you are to them, and engage them at the same time to keep peace, and simulate love among themselves till the moment when those little disputes shall not be attended with such inconveniences. It would be, too, a great pity that slavery, dishonour, ruin, and unhappiness of a whole world, should issue from some trifling differences between a few men.

You will find, perhaps, this letter very useless, and even inopportune; but I was desirous of having a pretty long conversation with you upon the present circumstances, to explain you what I think of this matter. As a proper opportunity for it did not occur, I took the liberty of laying down some of my ideas in this letter, because it is for my satisfaction to be convinced that you, my dear general, who have been indulgent enough to permit me to look on you as upon a friend, should know the confession of my sentiments in a matter which I consider as a very important one. I have the warmest love for my country and for every good Frenchman; their success fills my heart with joy; but, sir, besides, Conway is an Irishman, I want countrymen, who deserve, in every point, to do honour to their country. That gentleman had engaged me by entertaining my head with ideas of glory and shining projects, and I must confess, to my shame, that it is a too certain way of deceiving me.

I wished to join to the few theories about war I can have, and the few dispositions nature gave, perhaps, to me, the experience of thirty campaigns, in hope that I should be able to be the more useful in the present circumstances. My desire of deserving your satisfaction is stronger than ever, and everywhere you will employ me you can be certain of my

6

trying every exertion in my power to succeed. I am now fixed to your fate, and I shall follow it and sustain it as well by my sword as by all means in my power. You will pardon my importunity in favour of the sentiment which dictated it. Youth and friendship make me, perhaps, too warm, but I feel the greatest concern at all that has happened for some time since.

With the most tender and profound respect, I have the honour to be, &c.

FROM GENERAL WASHINGTON.

(ORIGINAL.)

Head-quarters, December 31st, 1777.

MY DEAR MARQUIS,—Your favour of yesterday conveyed to me fresh proof of that friendship and attachment, which I have happily experienced since the first of our acquaintance, and for which I entertain sentiments of the purest affection. It will ever constitute part of my happiness to know that I stand well in your opinion; because I am satisfied that you can have no views to answer by throwing out false colours, and that you possess a mind too exalted to condescend to low arts and intrigues to acquire a reputation. Happy, thrice happy, would it have been for this army and the cause we are embarked in, if the same generous spirit had pervaded all the actors in it. But one gentleman, whose name you have mentioned, had, I am confident, far different views; his ambition and great desire of being puffed off, as one of the first officers of the age, could only be equalled by the means which he used to obtain them. But finding that I was determined not to go beyond the line of my duty to indulge him in the first—nor to exceed the strictest rules of propriety to gratify him in the second—he became my inveterate enemy; and he has, I am persuaded, practised every art to do me an injury, even at the expense of reprobating a measure that did not succeed, that he himself advised to. How far he may have accomplished his ends, I know not; and except for considerations of a

7

public nature, I care not; for, it is well known, that neither ambitious nor lucrative motives, led me to accept my present appointments, in the discharge of which, I have endeavoured to observe one steady and uniform system of conduct, which I shall invariably pursue, while I have the honour to command, regardless of the tongue of slander, or the powers of detraction. The fatal tendency of disunion is so obvious, that I have, in earnest terms, exhorted such officers as have expressed their dissatisfaction at General Conway's promotion, to be cool and dispassionate in their decision about the matter; and I have hopes that they will not suffer any hasty determination to injure the service. At the same time, it must be acknowledged, that officers' feelings upon these occasions are not to be restrained, although you may control their actions.

The other observations contained in your letter have too much truth in them; and, it is much to be lamented, that things are not now as they formerly were. But we must not, in so great a contest, expect to meet with nothing but sunshine. I have no doubt that everything happens for the best, that we shall triumph over all our misfortunes, and, in the end, be happy; when, my dear marquis, if you will give me your company in Virginia, we will laugh at our past difficulties and the folly of others; and I will endeavour, by every civility in my power, to shew you how much, and how sincerely, I am your affectionate and obedient servant.

TO BARON DE STEUBEN.

(ORIGINAL—A FRAGMENT.)

Albany, March 12th.

PERMIT me to express my satisfaction at your having seen General Washington. No enemies to that great man can be found except among the enemies to his country; nor is it possible for any man of a noble spirit to refrain from loving the excellent qualities of his heart. I think I know him as well as any person, and such is the idea which I have formed of him; his honesty, his frankness, his sensibility, his virtue, to

8

the full extent in which this word can be understood, are above all praise. It is not for me to judge of his military talents; but, according to my imperfect knowledge of these matters, his advice in council has always appeared to me the best, although his modesty prevents him sometimes from sustaining it; and his predictions have generally been fulfilled. I am the more happy in giving you this opinion of my friend with all the sincerity which I feel, because some persons may perhaps attempt to deceive you on this point.

TO GENERAL WASHINGTON.

(ORIGINAL.)

Alliance, off Boston, December 21st, 1781.

MY DEAR GENERAL,—I am sorry to think we are not yet gone, and there still remain some doubts of our going to-morrow. This delay I lament not so much on private accounts as I do on the account of our next campaign, in the planning of which your opinion, as I shall deliver it, must be of the greatest use to the common cause. As to the department of foreign affairs, I shall be happy to justify the confidence of the congress, by giving my opinion to the best of my power, whenever it is asked for; but the affair of finances will, I fear, be a difficult point for the American minister, in which, however, I shall be happy to help him with my utmost exertions. The moment I arrive in France, I will write to you minutely how things stand, and give you the best accounts in my power.

I have received every mark of affection in Boston, and am much attached to this town, to which I owe so many obligations; but, from public considerations, I have been impatient to leave it and go on board the frigate, where I receive all possible civilities, but where I had rather be under sail than at anchor.

I beg your pardon, my dear general, for giving you so much trouble in reading my scrawls; but we are going to sail, and my last adieu, I must dedicate to my beloved general. Adieu, my dear general: I know your heart so well, that I am sure

9

that no distance can alter your attachment to me. With the same candour, I assure you that my love, my respect, my gratitude for you, are above expression; that, at the moment of leaving you, I felt more than ever the strength of those friendly ties that for ever bind me to you, and that I anticipate the pleasure, the most wished for pleasure, to be again with you, and, by my zeal and services, to gratify the feelings of my respect and affection. Will you be pleased to present my compliments and respects to Mrs. Washington, and to remember me to General Knox and General Lincoln.

Adieu, my dear general, your respectful and tender friend, &c.

FROM GENERAL WASHINGTON.

(ORIGINAL.)

Mount Vernon, December 8th, 1784.

MY DEAR MARQUIS,—The peregrinations of the day in which I parted from you, ended at Wailho. The next day, bad as it was, I got home before dinner. In the moment of our separation, upon the road as I travelled, and every hour since, I felt all that love, respect, and attachment for you, which length of years, and close connexion of your merits, have inspired me with. I often asked myself, as our carriages distanced, whether it was the last sight I ever should have of you, and though I wished to say no, my fears answered yes. I called to mind the days of my youth, and found they had long since fled to return no more; that I was now descending the hill I had seen diminishing for fifty-two years, and though I was blessed with a good constitution, I was of a short-lived family, and might soon expect to be entombed in the dreary mansions of my fathers. These things darkened the horizon, and gave a gloom to the future, consequently to my prospects of seeing you again. But I will not repine: I have had my day. Nothing of importance has occurred since I parted with you. I found my family well, and am now immersed in company; notwithstanding which I have, in haste, produced a few more letters to give you the trouble of, rather inclining to commit them to your care than to place them in many and unknown hands. It is unnecessary, I persuade myself, to repeat to you, my dear marquis, the sincerity of my regard and friendship: nor have I words which could express my affection for you were I to attempt it. My fervent prayers are offered for your safe and pleasant passage, happy meeting with Madame Lafayette and family, and the completion of every wish of your heart; in all which Mrs. Washington joins me, as she does in compliments to Captain Grandchain and the chevalier, of whom little Washington often speaks. With every sentiment which is propitious and endearing, I am, &c.

TO GENERAL WASHINGTON.

(ORIGINAL.)

On board the *Nymph,* New York harbour,
December 21, 1784.

MY DEAR GENERAL,—I have received your affectionate letter of the 8th instant, and from the known sentiments of my heart, you will easily guess what my feelings have been in perusing the tender expressions of your friendship. No, my dear general, our late parting was not by any means a last interview. My whole soul revolts at the idea, and could I harbour it an instant, indeed, my dear general it would make me miserable. I well see you never will go to France: the inexpressible pleasure of embracing you in my own house, of welcoming you in a family where your name is adored, I do not much expect to experience; but to you I shall return, and within the walls of Mount Vernon we shall yet often speak of old times. My firm plan is to visit now and then my friends on this side of the Atlantic, and the most beloved of all friends I ever had or ever shall have anywhere, is too strong an inducement for me to return to him, not to think that whenever it is possible I shall renew my so pleasing visits to Mount Vernon.

Since I have left you, my dear general, we have passed through Philadelphia to Trenton, where I was happy to find

11

a numerous and well chosen congress. Their testimonies of kindness to me, and my answer to them, you will see in the newspapers. As to my services abroad, it has been (on motion respecting what I told you) universally decided that public confidence in me was a matter of course, a doubt of which ought not to be expressed; but as I know the sense of congress, and as Mr. Jay* has accepted, and Mr. Jefferson will be minister in France, my situation in that respect will be very agreeable.

Orders have been sent to Canada to reinforce the posts, put the lake vessels in commission, and repel force by force; but I think that if once congress have the trade to regulate, mercantile interdictions will set those people to rights. Although party spirit has a little subsided in New York, yet that city is not by any means settled. How far from Boston!

Although your nephew is not arrived, I still hope for the pleasure to see him in Paris. General Greene was in Hartford when the letter reached him, from whence he came to New York, and I had the pleasure to spend some days with him. Inclosed I send you a small cypher. Should any public political business require a fuller one, I will write to you by a complete cypher, which I have had long ago with Mr. Jay's present department.

Mr. Cary, printer of the Volunteer Journal, has been obliged to fly for his life, and now lives at Mr. Sutter's, hatter, front street in Philadelphia, where he is going to set up a paper. A letter from you, becoming a subscriber, and telling him I have mentioned it to you, will the more oblige me, as I have promised him to recommend him to my friends: he now is an *American,* and we have nothing to do with his quarrel with the Duke of Rutland, which disputes, by the bye, seem to subside and to vanish into nothing. The French packet is not yet arrived.

Chevalier de Caraman and Captain Grandchain beg leave to offer their respects to you, Mrs. Washington, and all the

* Mr. Jay was named secretary of state for foreign affairs.

family. My most affectionate, tender respects wait upon Mrs. Washington; I beg she will give a kiss for me to the little girls, my friend Tub; and I beg Mrs. Stuart, the Doctor, Mr. Lund Washington, and all our friends, to receive my best compliments. I hope Mr. Harrison will be soon appointed, and I wish his cousin may know it.

Adieu, adieu, my dear general: it is with inexpressible pain that I feel I am going to be severed from you by the Atlantic. Everything that admiration, respect, gratitude, friendship, and filial love, can inspire, is combined in my affectionate heart to devote me most tenderly to you. In your friendship I find a delight which words cannot express. Adieu, my dear general; it is not without emotion that I write this word, although I know I shall soon visit you again. Be attentive to your health. Let me hear from you every month. Adieu, adieu.

Duponceau

Pierre-Etienne Duponceau, born at Saint-Martin-de-Ré, in 1750, came over to America in 1777, as aide-de-camp to Baron de Steuben. After the war he settled in America, became a very prominent citizen of Philadelphia where he died in 1844. Some of his letters have been printed under the title of *Autobiographical Letters of Peter S. Duponceau*. Pennsylvania Magazine of History and Biography. Vol. 40, 1916. A complete edition has recently appeared in the same publication from April 1939 through April 1940, with an introduction and notes by James L. Whitehead. The following passages are reproduced here by the kind permission of the editor.

WASHINGTON AT VALLEY FORGE

Philadelphia 13th June 1836.

MY DEAR SIR

On our journey to Valley Forge we passed through Lancaster, then, considered the largest inland town in the United States. Having arrived there early in the afternoon, the Baron

13

was waited upon by Colonel Gibson and other gentlemen, who invited him, and his family, to a Subscription Ball, to take place that evening. The Baron accepted, and we accordingly went. There we saw assembled, all the fashion and beauty of Lancaster, and its vicinity. The Baron was delighted to converse with the German girls in his native tongue. There was a handsome supper, and the company did not separate until two o'clock the next morning.

From Lancaster, we proceeded directly to Valley-Forge, where we arrived on the 23ᵈ of February. On the next day, I had the honor of being presented to Gen¹ Washington, and to dine with him that day, and the next. He received the Baron with great cordiality, and to me he shewed much condescending attention. I cannot describe the impression, that the first sight of that great man made upon me. I could not keep my eyes from that imposing countenance; grave, yet not severe; affable, without familiarity. Its predominant expression was calm dignity, through which you could trace the strong feelings of the patriot, and discern the father, as well as the commander of his soldiers. I have never seen a picture, that represents him to me, as I saw him at Valley-Forge, and during the campaigns in which I had the honour to follow him. Perhaps that expression was beyond the skill of the painter; but while I live it will remain impressed on my memory. I had frequent opportunities of seeing him, as it was my duty to accompany the Baron when he dined with him, which was sometimes twice or thrice in the same week. We visited him also in the evening, when Mʳˢ Washington was at Head-quarters. We were in a manner domesticated in the family.

General Washington had three aids; Tench Tilghman, John Laurens, and Alexander Hamilton. Robert Hanson Harrison was his Secretary. I soon formed a friendship with Laurens, and Hamilton, as well as with Major Monroe, then Aid de Camp to Lord Stirling, and since President of the United States. With Harrison and Tilghman, I had but a common acquaintance. Laurens was master of several

14

languages. I have a letter from him in Latin, Greek, English, French, and Spanish. With Monroe I corresponded almost daily, although our quarters were little distant from each other. After his elevation to the Presidency, he wrote me a long letter, expressive of his remembrance of our former friendship. Had I been ambitious of places, here was a fine opportunity offered me to obtain that end; but I preferred my independence, and suffered that opportunity to pass unimproved.

The situation of our Army, during the dismal winter that we spent at Valley-Forge, has been so often described, and by none in more vivid colours, than by Washington himself, in his letters written at that time, and which may be seen in Mr. Spark's collection, that I shall forbear to expatiate upon the subject. Suffice it to say that we were in want of provisions, of clothes, of fodder for our horses, in short of everything. I remember seeing the soldiers, popping their heads out of their miserable huts, and calling out in an under tone, "No bread, no soldier." Their condition was truly pitiful; and their courage and perseverance is beyond all praise. We, who lived in good quarters, did not feel the misery of the times, so much as the common soldiers, and the subaltern officers; yet we had more than once to share our rations with the sentry at our door. We put the best face we could upon the matter. Once, with the Baron's permission, his aids invited a number of young officers, to dine at our quarters; on condition that none should be admitted, that had on a whole pair of breeches. This, was of course, understood as *pars pro toto;* but torn clothes were an indispensable requisite for admission; and in this, the guests were very sure not to fail. The dinner took place; the guests clubbed their rations, and we feasted sumptuously on tough beef-steaks, and potatoes, with hickory nuts for our dessert. In lieu of wine, we had some kind of spirits, with which we made *Salamanders;* that is to say, : after filling our glasses, we set the liquor on fire, and drank it up, flame and all. Such a set of ragged, and at the same time merry fellows, were never brought together. The Baron loved to speak of that dinner, and of his *Sans-Culottes,* as he called us. Thus, this denomination was first invented in America, and applied to the brave officers, and soldiers of our revolutionary army; at a time when it could not be foreseen; that the name which honored the followers of Washington, would afterwards be assumed by the satellites of a Marat, and a Robespierre.

In the midst of all our distress, there were some bright sides to the picture, which Valley-Forge exhibited at that time. Mrs. Washington had the courage to follow her husband in that dismal abode; other ladies also graced the scene. Among them, was the lady of General Greene, a handsome, elegant, and accomplished woman. Her dwelling was the resort of the foreign officers, because she understood, and spoke the French language, and was well versed in French literature. There were also Lady Stirling, the wife of Major General Lord Stirling; her daughter, Lady Kitty Alexander, who afterwards married Mr Wm Duer of New York; and her companion Miss Nancy Brown, then a distinguished belle. There was Mrs. Biddle, the wife of Colonel Clement Biddle, who was at the head of the forage department, and some other ladies whose names I do not at present recollect. They often met at each other's quarters, and sometimes at General Washington's, where the evening was spent in conversation, over a dish of tea or coffee. There were no *levees* or formal *soirees;* no dancing, card-playing, or amusement of any kind, except singing. Every gentleman or lady who could sing, was called upon in turn for a song. As I had a tolerable voice, and some knowledge of music, I found myself of consequence in these *reunions.* I soon learned the favorite English songs, and contributed my share to the pleasures of the company.

Thus the time passed, until the beginning of May, when the news of the French Alliance burst suddenly upon us. Then the public distress was forgotten amidst the universal joy: I shall never forget that glorious time. I was not yet an American: I was proud of being a Frenchman. Rejoicings

16

took place throughout the army; toasts, songs, *feux de joie* and what not? I thought I should be devoured by the caresses which the American officers lavished upon me, as one of their new allies. Wherever a French officer appeared, he was met with congratulations, and with smiles. O! that was a delightful time! It bound me forever to the country of my adoption.

The six weeks that elapsed after the reception of this news, passed amidst the hopes and the dreams of future triumphs. The British evacuated Philadelphia on the 18th of June, and I entered it on the same day.

While we were at Valley-Forge, Baron Steuben was appointed a Major General, and Inspector General of the armies of the United States. To the post of his secretary, which I then held, he was pleased to add that of his aid-de-camp, which gave me, by courtesy, the rank of Major, which I preserved until I quitted the military service.

I remain Very Sincerely

Your friend and humble Servant.

Philadelphia 24th June 1836.

My Dear Sir:

I forgot to mention in my last letter, that it was at Valley-Forge, that I became acquainted with Gen¹ Lafayette, on his return from Albany; the intended expedition against Canada not having taken place. He showed from the first much partiality to me; which afterwards ripened into a friendship, that ceased but with his life.

I ought also to have mentioned, that before we left Valley-Forge, the Baron took another Aid-de-Camp into his family. It was Captain Benjamin Walker, who afterwards was aid to Gen¹ Washington. He was an Englishman by birth, and had been brought up for the counting house. He had not received a brilliant, but a solid education; he was master of the French language; and was gifted by nature, with a clear head, and a sound judgment. He was brave, intelligent, honest, and true. I enjoyed his friendship to the time of his death. The Baron was very much attached to him, and left him heir to

17

one half of his property. He died at Utica, some years afterwards, beloved and respected by all who knew him.

While I am on the subject of this gentleman, I must relate an anecdote which happened while he was in the family of Gen[l] Washington, and which is strongly descriptive of his honest heart. He had long been engaged to a Quaker young lady, who resided in the State of New York, and whom he afterwards married. He once asked the General to give him leave of absence for a few days, to go and see her. The General told him, that he could not at that time dispense with his services. Walker insisted, begged, entreated, but all in vain. "If I don't go," said he, "she will die." "Oh! no," said Washington, "women do not die for such trifles." "But, General, what shall I do?" "What you will do? why write to her to add another leaf to the *book of sufferings*." This was related to me by Walker himself. Gen[l] Washington had a great deal of that dry humour, which he knew how to make use of on proper occasions. But I must return to my narrative.

A VISIT TO MOUNT VERNON IN 1780

. . . We parted with General Greene somewhere in the State of Delaware and pursued our route to Richmond in Virginia. On our way the Baron (de Steuben) paid a visit to Mrs. Washington at Mount Vernon; we were most cordially received and invited to dinner. The external appearance of the mansion did not strike the Baron very favourably "if" said he "Washington were not a better general than he was an architect the affairs of America would be in a very bad condition." The house at that time might be considered handsome and perhaps elegant but at present the most that can be said of it is that it is a modest habitation, quite in keeping with the idea we have of Cincinnatus and of those other great commanders of the Roman Republic. Such is the idea that I formed of it at the time. In the interior we saw only two rooms separated by an entry, one of which was a parlour, the

18

other the dining room. They were respectably but not luxuriously furnished.

The Baron having accepted the invitation we sat down to dinner. Mrs. Washington was accompanied by a young lady, a relative, whose name, I think, was Miss Custis. The table was abundantly served, but without profusion. If I were Mr. Hamilton, the celebrated writer of Men and Manners in America, I could describe in detail all the dishes that were set before us, and tell you how they looked and how they tasted; but, alas! I paid no great attention to them as I was restricted to a severe diet and they have escaped from my memory. I can only say that I saw there for the first time *preserved strawberries* whether that kind of sweetmeats was then not so common in France as in this country, or whatever may be the cause, I had never seen any before. Those were large and beautiful, and I indulged in eating a few of them. I have been fond of them ever since.

After dinner was over, while the Baron and Major Walker in company with the young lady were viewing the grounds I had the honour of sitting in the parlour tête-à-tête with Mrs. Washington. I shall never forget the affability, and, at the same time, the dignity of her demeanour. Our conversation was on general subjects. I can only remember the impression it left upon my mind; she reminded me of the Roman matrons of whom I had read so much, and I thought that she well deserved to be the companion and friend of the greatest man of the age.

Duportail

On Duportail, see the excellent and well documented study of Miss Elizabeth Kite: *Brigadier-General Louis Lebègue Duportail. Commandant of Engineers in the Continental Army, 1777-1783*. Baltimore, The Johns Hopkins Press. 1933 The extract given here was written in French and translated into English by Colonel John Laurens in answer to a circular letter sent by Washington to the American generals in camp, April 20, 1778. It was published in full by Miss Kite, p. 60-71. The letter written by Duportail to Washington after returning to France is given in the original English of the writer. (Kite, p. 275-277).

REPORT OF DUPORTAIL TO WASHINGTON (1778)

What we ought to propose ourselves, is to defend the country inch by inch, to endeavor to hinder the enemy from rendering himself master of it, consequently never to receive him but when we are protected by a natural or artificial fortification, in other words to carry on what is styled a *defensive War*. this is our true part and it is so obvious that in Europe, all Military men and even those who are not so, suppose this to be our Conduct—if the Americans could consult the modern daily publications, they should there find that the model offered to General Washington is principally Fabius, that wise Roman who ruined Hannibal by refusing to fight him in plain. Fabius however commanded Romans, but these Romans had been thrice defeated, they were disheartened, dreaded the Enemy, and were nearly reduced to the condition of new and unformed Troops. The Consul conducted himself accordingly, avoided general Battles, kept himself on the defensive, always occupying strong positions and where the Enemy could not attack him but with considerable disadvantage—it is true that this kind of war was not approved of at Rome; Men of leisure who loved to be amused by great events, men of impetuous dispositions, men whose discernment was not sufficient to judge of what circumstances required, in a word the particular enemies of the Consul, turned him into ridicule, affixed to him insulting surnames, but the sage General was unmoved by them. he knew that after all, the event would determine his reputation in the world—he therefore invariably pursued his plan, and by his firmness which was crowned with success,, he merited the appellation of Savior of Rome.

DUPORTAIL TO WASHINGTON

paris 24 dec. 1783

DEAR GENERAL

i arrived here ten days ago from London; i landed at plymouth, traveled through England about three hundred miles and stayed at london five days; i intended to stay sometime longer but was prevented by different news i heard from here—your excellency will not be surprised of that *tour* of mine after the american war it was certainly curious to see england & to observe the effect of their misfortunes the alterations it ought to produce in their government and so for those reasons i propose to return there in two months hence there is now in that city and throughout the country another cause of fermentation. it is the affair of the east indies. as you receive probably the english papers i thinck it superfluous to give your excellency any account of it—but i will be satisfied with saying to you that after all that i heard of the situation of their affairs in that part of the world, it is a great pity that france has made peace with england so for one year more and probably they were irrevocably lost there. it is what i imagined while in america—i cannot give you any interesting news from this place. pleasure, diversions are the first objects which strike the attention here and the person arriving should thinck that there are no other affairs in paris. to know that it is not so requires some stay so as i cannot give you anything interesting in politics i am almost tempted to give you something in the physical way but i suppose this same ship will carry you from every one of your correspondents great particulars about the *merveille* of the time. your excellency conceives that i am speaking of the air baloon the most extraordinary discovery ever made but in that very matter i am pretty ignorant; i had not yet time since i am here of penetrating into all the proceedings. Chv. de Chastellux to whom i delivered your letter told me that he intended to give your excellency an account of it. nobody can do it better than that gentleman.

everybody here, dear general, asks me if you intend to come over—i give them little hope after what you told me. your excellency may be certain that he would be received in france with great pleasure but no body could have a greater satisfaction to see you than myself—you may be an object of admiration from those who are at a distance and who know only your military and political life but for those who are so happy as to be particularly acquainted with your excellency's private character you are equally an object of veneration and attachment—however if i have little hopes of seeing you in france i hope to see you in america for i am far from renouncing from that country forever. may be i shall be able to tell you more about it a few weeks hence. i suppose this letter will find your excellency in Virginia. permit me to present my respects to Mrs Washington and my compliments to the gentlemen our companions in the war who are so happy as to live near you. i have the honor to be etc.

DUPORTAIL

Gouvion

An account of Jean Baptiste Gouvion and his complete "états de service" will be found in Commandant André Lasseray's book: *Les Français sous les Treize Etoiles*. Paris, 1935. Vol. I, p. 234. Born in 1747, first lieutenant in the army of the King in 1771, he came over with Duportail. He died while serving under Lafayette before Maubeuge, in 1792, and his name was inscribed on the Arc de Triomphe. The letter here given was published by Miss Kite, *op. cit.*, p. 275.

GOUVION TO WASHINGTON

SIR

At the moment of leaving this country where I had the honour of serving for seven years under your command, I beg your Excellency's leave to express to you how grateful I am for all the favours which you have been pleased to bestow upon me. Although the part I acted in this happy and glorious revolution was but small, I shall always take pride in remembering that I was an American officer. The testimonies I have of the satisfaction your Excellency had of my services will in every time be dear to me. they were my only wish and I feel very happy in having obtained them.

May your Excellency experience from his country a gratitude so well deserved, but which can never be equal to the unparalleled toils, labours, and cares you have sustained to save it, may you for a long while see its inhabitants enjoy . . . happiness and prosperity.

I have the honor to be etc. . . .

J. GOUVION

Philadelphia, nov. 4th 1783.

Colonel Armand

Armand-Charles Tuffin, Marquis de la Rouërie, born April 13, 1750 in Brittany is described by Moré de Pontgibaud and Chateaubriand for whom he wrote a letter of introduction to Washington. He came over at the end of 1776, and was authorized by Washington to raise a "corps franc" of dragoons. He was one of the most brilliant cavalrymen of the War of Independence and died in 1793. See Commandant Lasseray, vol. II, p. 454-462. Mr. Fernand Baldensperger is preparing a new edition of his letters, published for the first time under the title of : *Letters of Col. Armand (Marquis de la Rouerie) 1777-1791.* Collections of the New York Historical Society for the year 1878. New York, 1879.

ARMAND DISBANDS HIS LEGION
TO GENERAL WASHINGTON

Philadelphia N^bre *29*^th *1783*

. . . it gives me much pain not to have been able to disband the legion the 15th as you had ordered, because your Excellency not having perhaps a perfect knowledge of me might suppose

that the war being at an end & myself near to quit the country,
I give less importance to my punctuality in obeying your commands—if such were your thoughts permit me to request here
your Excellency to make in them that alteration which my
heart full of respect and attachment for you do really deserve—though perhaps I may never be so happy as to bear
again a commission under your command, I am too sensible
of your superiority over men in general and your past kindness
to me act with too much force on my feelings for me not
to be submitted to you all my days & in all occasions whatever—I regret to have not fought & not to fight for a cause
more personal to his Excellency, general Washington—happi
indeed would I be at the instant where sheding all my blood,
my soul leaving this world would glorify with the honor
of having served my heroe—but I am not so fortunate &
allready to far in my career to change my profession. I am
perhaps doomed to serve a man out of my choice, however
I will have the encouragement in my future life, that by a
propriety in my conduct I am assured to deserve and obtain
your esteem. . . .

Armand Mqs de la Rouerie.

THE MOTHER OF ARMAND TO
GENERAL WASHINGTON

Rouerie 12th Jany 1784

"translation"

Will the heroe of our age, the man of all ages, the object
of the admiration of all the nations & particularly of france,
the theme of true enthusiasm, will the Great Washington
allow a french woman, a native of Britanny, too aspiring perhaps, but still more an admirer of that commanding character,
to join with a feeble voice in that tribute of praise which every
one pays to that Great Man—Some compare him to Cezar,
others to trajan, to Alexander, to fabius, to turenne & to
Catinat among the ancients, & they take the talents & virtues
of modern Characters, in order to form out of them a Great

24

Whole, here their art fails, forgive this familiar Language, it is that in which we address the Gods.

Washington, I have a son, he leaves thee, he has served under thy Command, fought under thy Eyes, thou knowest him, thou doest more, thou honorest him with thy Esteem, impart those flattering sentiments to our Ministers, the opinions of such a man as thou art hath an ascendency which gives it the force of a law. What a title thy approbation ensures? he who hath acquired it hath obtained a right to that of every other Person.

May the Parcae spare the thread of thy Glorious Days which are so precious to Posterity, such is the ardent wish formed for the sake of Both, by the humblest of thy servants

The Mother of Armand

His Excellency G^{rl} Washington.

ARMAND CONGRATULATES WASHINGTON ON HIS ELECTION TO THE PRESIDENCY

TO GENERAL WASHINGTON

la Rouerie par Fougeres in Bretagne
June 18th 89.

SIR,

I had the honour of writing to your Excellency by Mr. de Bert an ancient captain of the Legion I had the happyness to command in your army—that gentleman was going to settle and live in your country, it was a good opportunity for my heart since it was a man for whom I have a great esteem which I intrusted with the care of the expressions and protestations of my unlimited sentiments of respect, veneration, gratitude, permit me, Sir, to say, tenderness for your Excellency. Mr de Bert has had since some family affaires which have detained him in france six months more, & perhaps you will receive this letter before the one which he has taken the charge of.

We have had the confirmation that you are by your post at the head of affaires; in my former letter to your Excellency

25

73987

I complimented your country on that event, which surely will be like all those where circumstances have permitted you to be concerned in, the most advantageous & dear to America & the most renowned in her history—as to you, Sir, I do not think you have had any promotion—your influence over your country men & in public affaires and in the many services & virtues which gave it to you, had placed and maintained you upon that mighty eminence from which the man who happen to be Born every three or four hundred years, look down with a holy pride and tranquility upon kings, & great dignitary while individuals & nations look up with respect and admiration to that man and regret, for the happyness & honor of humanity, he does not command over the whole world.

ᏔMoré de Pontgibaud

Born in Clermont (Puy-de- Dôme), in 1758, de Pontgibaud came over to America after escaping from a prison where he had been confined by his family's orders. His memoirs published under the title of *Mémoires du Comte de M., précédés de cinq lettres, ou considérations sur les mémoires particuliers,* Paris, 1828, were translated and edited by Robert Douglas, Paris 1897 and reprinted several times in New York. They are almost as entertaining as Dumas' *Mémoires du comte de Monte-Christo*. For his biography, see Lasseray, I, p. 320.

FIRST MEETING WITH WASHINGTON

At last I reached Valley Forge in the last days of November. The American army was encamped at a distance of three or four leagues from the English army which occupied Philadelphia.

As soon as I discovered the map, my imagination represented an army, uniforms, all the brilliant apparel of arms and flags, in a word all the aspects of military life. Instead

of the magnificent display I expected, I found militia men
scattered or in groups, badly clad, most of them without shoes,
a great number poorly armed, but all of them tolerably well
fed. I noticed that tea and sugar were regularly issued to
them. As I did not know that it was the custom, I could not
help laughing remembering our recruiting sergeants on the
Quai de la Ferraille advertising to the boys they wanted to
enroll: "Life in the regiment is very comfortable, not only
you will not eat hard-tack but you must resign yourself to a
diet of cake." Here indeed the soldiers had tea and sugar.
While I was advancing through the camp I noticed another
contrast: some soldiers wore a hat and in addition a sort of
night-cap; some were using as cloaks and overcoats woollen
blankets similar to those worn by the patients in our French
hospitals. I realized a little later that those were officers and
generals.

Such were, exactly described on the day when I saw them
for the first time, the costume and appearance of this population under arms whose leader was the man who soon was to
make famous the name of Washington. Such were these
colonists from every rank of life, unexperienced soldiers who,
in a few years learned how to defeat the best soldiers of the
British monarchy; such was the misery of the insurgent army;
such, finally, in these hesitating beginnings of the War of
Independence, was the need of money and the feeble resources
of this government now so rich, so powerful and so prosperous, when its money called continental paper money was
practically worthless and only comparable to the assignats
we were to know in 1795.

Under these impressions which corresponded so imperfectly
to the illusions I had entertained, I proceeded through this
queer army and arrived at the headquarters of M. le Marquis
de la F[ayette].

This young general was then, I believe, only twenty or
twenty-one. I introduced myself and told him frankly my
whole story. He listened kindly and at my request accepted
me as a volunteer. He wrote to France and it was not long

27

before he received confirmation of all I had told him. He then admitted me among his aides - de - camp with a commission of major, and from that time on showed me constantly the greatest kindness and confidence.

The Marquis de la F . . . introduced me as his aide-de-camp to the General-in-chief. The General was one of these master pieces of nature who inspire respect and confidence at first sight and are gifted with all the external attributes which make them born leaders. He was tall, his face was commanding, his eyes were kind, his language gracious, his gestures and words simple and above all a calm and firm behaviour harmonized all these qualities. I was seeing and hearing Washington. This general, since become so famous by his talents and successes was just assuming the historical part which he was to play so gloriously for many years in military, civil and political life; but I shall speak of him only as a general. He was surrounded with his officers, most of them entering as I was upon their first campaign; but several were to derive from a sort of military instinct and from love of liberty an intuitive science and glory. Several of them were far from suspecting that they were to be called to a military career. Around the General, I saw Gates, the victor of Saratoga; only two years before that battle, he was a good and prosperous farmer, a man of short stature and about fifty. Such was the man who, unknowingly, already belonged to history; such was the ploughman become a soldier who with his woollen cap topped by a farmer's hat upon his head had just received the sword of dashing General Burgoyne, clad in his dress uniform covered with all the orders of England. Next was Arnold, as brave as he was treacherous, who was to limp for the rest of his life from a shot received at Saratoga while sharing the dangers and the glory of General Gates. A few months before becoming a well-known chief in the army, General Arnold was but a horse dealer. General Lee was a soldier before the War of Independence. General Sullivan was a lawyer: after the signature of the treaty of peace he went back not to his plough but to his law office. When the

28

war was over, Colonel Hamilton, Washington's friend, became a lawyer and practiced in Philadelphia. General Stark used to be a land owner tilling his land. Brave General Knox, who was a bookseller before the insurrection, commanded the artillery. Under him served young Duplessis-Mauduit, then about twenty-six, a brave officer I shall have occasion to mention often, who died at Santo Domingo cowardly murdered by his own soldiers.

I also saw arriving at the general headquarters, which by the way were a mill, Colonel Armand, who was in charge of some light cavalry. This young Frenchman then twenty-four years old was pursuing a career which like mine was to be very adventurous and had already been very stormy. An officer in the Gardes Françaises, a nephew of Marquis de la Belinaie, the desperate lover of Mademoiselle Beaumesnil of the Opera, he had first entered the monastery of La Trappe, then had left it in order to risk his life under General Washington. Under the name of Colonel Armand he had already found glory: thus the famous Marquis de la Rouairie was already making himself known.

Finally, there I saw, for the first time, M. Du Portail who commanded the engineers and who since became minister of war under the monarchy and King Louis XVI at the beginning of the Revolution.

Among all these officers, representing nations and ways of life so different, I was wondering who was the noble looking person to whom all paid obedience spontaneously as well as out of duty. I was wondering what sort of a man was Washington himself. He was then about forty; he had served in the English army; he was the same major Washington who commanded in 175.. at Fort Necessity, when M. de Jumonville, a French officer and a bearer of a flag of truce was assassinated through the most deplorable misunderstanding. It stands as a fact in the tradition of the country that M. de Jumonville was killed, through the mistake, the fault, the individual act of a soldier who shot him, whether he knew or not that he was coming under a flag of truce; but I repeat that

29

it is accepted as a fact in the tradition of the country, that the commander of the fort did not give the order to shoot; the most unimpeachable evidence being the moderate, magnanimous and kind character of General Washington which has never varied amidst the various trials of war and the utmost of good or bad fortune. Mr. Thomas has thought it more poetical and more patriotic to represent this episode under colors most detrimental to the British officer. The name of major Washington would have gone down into history obscurely but under an abominable suspicion. Nobody would have taken any interest in destroying it; but any attempt to discuss it would be an insult to one of the most beautiful and noblest characters in the known world. All suspicions must disappear before the name, the virtues and the glory of General Washington: the murderer of Jumonville could never have become a great man.

At the time of the insurrection, George Washington was a rich Virginia planter, and as such he had brought with him to the army a large number of magnificent horses. Clad in the simplest uniform, without any distinctive indication of his rank, he gave much to the soldiers who loved him, but he gave out of his own patrimony, for he did not receive, nor did he wish to receive any salary from the government.

I must say here, much to the indeniable glory of M. le Marquis de La Fayette, that following the example of the general in chief, he spent very generously, buying with his own money all that could be found to equip and arm his soldiers. This war has cost him enormous sums of money; and he cannot be suspected of any selfish motive except the noble motive of acquiring some glory, for the chances for being repaid were not very probable. It is certain that everything was above suspicion in his noble sacrifices which can be explained only through the prestige that liberty or chivalry will always enjoy in France. Enthusiasm, love of dangers, a modicum of glory were his only compensation. The pleasure to be in command, to make war, to become famous weighed in his mind also to a certain degree; it is not unreasonable to calculate, but it is honorable and creditable to calculate in a noble manner. Also, at that time, when the American cause offered only dangers without glory, privations, fatigues, difficulties of all sorts, M. le Marquis de La Fayette was the only young nobleman from the court of France who had the initiative and the courage to give up pleasures and palaces and to travel 1800 leagues in order to speculate in a glory which could bring any other reward.

Even then, General Washington did not provide every day an opportunity to acquire glory; it was not in his plans to engage the enemy without due consideration. He expected everything from time and from the faults of those he had made it his business to fight, to nibble and to destroy. Armed temporisation was his constant care and it was only justice to call him the American Fabius: the event has consecrated the name. (*Editor's translation*. Moré, pp. 109-117.)

II.

Rochambeau
and the French Army Officers

ROCHAMBEAU
SÉGUR
MATHIEU DUMAS
GUILLAUME DE DEUX-PONTS
CHASTELLUX
FERSEN
CLAUDE BLANCHARD
ABBÉ ROBIN

Rochambeau

Rochambeau's memoirs were published in 1809 as *Mémoires militaires, historiques et politiques du Maréchal comte de Rochambeau,* 2 vols. Paris, and translated into English in part under the title of *Memoirs of the Marshal Count de Rochambeau relative to the War of Independence,* Paris 1838. The passage reproduced here is taken from that edition, p. 104, 105. Rochambeau wrote with a military brevity and could be even more reserved on his personal affairs and feelings than Washington himself. He discussed Washington's character only once, on the occasion of the signature of the peace treaty. On his biography, see *Rochambeau Father and Son,* by Jean-Edmond Weelen. New York, 1936.

WASHINGTON DISBANDS HIS ARMY

The glorious peace, of such import to America, was proclaimed shortly afterwards. General Washington, at the head of an army to which nearly seven years' arrears of pay was due, found it no easy task to satisfy its demands with paper money, when its disbanding was talked of. An insurrection broke out amongst the troops, who persisted in maintaining themselves as a corps, and in *statu quo,* until the amount of pay should be acquitted in full by the different States in their respective shares. General Washington, with that noble and patriotic character which ever formed the basis of his conduct, used his influential power over the minds of his soldiers to bring them round to those feelings of generosity with which they had been animated in the whole course of the Revolution. It was at his instigation that the Cincinnatus association was proposed, to commemorate the alliance of France, as an

35

indissoluble bond of their mutual fraternity, and an honourable mark of their services. Having at last accomplished the disbanding of his army, he took leave of his military career by a letter which depicts with admirable precision the character of this great man, and which will certainly be handed down to posterity in the history of every country.

Comte de Ségur

Louis-Philippe, comte de Ségur, son of the Marquis who was Minister of War under Louis XVI, from 1780 to 1787. Ségur did not emigrate; he served under Napoleon and Louis XVIII and died in 1830. For his biography see: Baron Ludovic de Contenson, *La Société des Cincinnati de France,* Paris, 1934. In 1859 were published his *Mémoires, souvenirs et anecdotes par M. le Comte de Ségur,* 2 vols.; an abridged translation by Gerard Shelley appeared in New York in 1928.

SEGUR MEETS WASHINGTON AT WEST POINT

One of my most earnest wishes was to see the hero of America, General Washington. He was then encamped a short distance from us and M. de Rochambeau was kind enough to present me to him. Too often reality is far below imagination, and admiration decreases on seeing at close range the person admired; but when I beheld General Washington I found a perfect accord between the impression made by his appearance and the idea I had entertained of him.

His presence almost foretold his history: simplicity, grandeur, dignity, calm, kindness, firmness were stamped upon his face and upon his countenance as well as his character. His figure was noble and tall; the expression on his face was pleasant and kind; his smile was gentle, his manners simple without being familiar.

He did not flaunt the magnificence displayed by generals under our monarchies; he was the embodiment of the repulican hero. He inspired rather than commanded respect and in the eyes of all the men around him one could read their real affection and whole-hearted confidence in a chief upon whom they seemed to rely entirely for their security. His headquarters at some distance from the camp, were an image of the order which prevailed in his life, in his habits and his conduct.

I had expected to see in this democratic camp unkempt soldiers and officers without training, all republicans devoid of this urbanity so common in our old civilized countries. I recalled the first days of their revolution, when ploughmen and artisans who had never handled a gun had rushed on without any semblance of order, in the name of their country, in order to give battle to the British phalanxes astonished at the sight of this mob of rustics without any military insignia except a cap on which was written the word *Liberty*.

One may imagine how surprized I was when I saw a well-disciplined army presenting in every detail the very image of order, reason, training and experience. The generals, their aides-de-camp and the other officers evidenced in their behavior and their speech noble and decent manners and a natural kindness which in my opinion is just as much superior to politeness as a gentle face is superior to a mask which one has striven to make pleasant.

This dignity in every individual, this self respect which sprung from their love of liberty and their feeling of equality had not constituted small obstacles to the chief who had to rise above them without awakening jealousy and who had to bend their independence to discipline without stirring discontent.

Any other man but Washington would have failed in the undertaking; it will suffice to say in order to appreciate his genius and wisdom that, in the midst of a stormy revolution, for seven years he was in command of the army of a free people without arousing fear in his country or distrust in Congress.

In every circumstance, he united the approbation of the destitute and the wealthy, of magistrates and soldiers; finally

37

he is perhaps the only man who has conducted and brought to an end a civil war without exposing himself to a single well founded reproach. As every one knew that he counted for nothing his own personal interest and that general interest was his only aim, he enjoyed while still living the unanimous recognition that contemporaries usually refuse to grant to the greatest men and which they must expect only from posterity. One might have said that envy seeing him placed in such a lofty position had become discouraged and powerless because it had no hope to wound him with any of its darts.

When I saw him, General Washington was forty nine years of age; with great modesty, he strove to avoid the tributes which people were delighted to offer him; and yet no man ever knew better how to acknowledge them and to respond to them. He used to listen with kind attention to those who addressed him and the expression upon his face answered even before his very words.

He was still very young when he started upon his military career and fought against France on the Canadian border, at the head of Virginia militiamen. After he returned home, this man who was to play such an important part in his country, remained inactive in his house for a long time, apparently preferring a philosophical rest to the agitation of public affairs.

Devoid of ambition, he participated but little in the first incidents which marked the American insurrection; but as soon as war was irrevocably declared, when the State and the Army were in need of a leader, everyone looked up to Washington whose wisdom was generally acknowledged; it must be added that in a country which had been at peace for so long, he was perhaps at the time the only man who had any idea and any memory of war.

Impelled by the purest and the most disinterested love of his country, he refused to receive the salary which was assigned to him as general in chief and it was almost against his wishes that he accepted to have the Nation assume his table expenses. At his table thirty people sat everyday. These meals, according to the English and American custom, lasted several hours and ended with many toasts, most of them to the independence of the United States, to the King and Queen of France, the success of the allied armies; then came the individual toasts, or as one used to say in America, toasts of sentiments.

Almost always when the table had been cleared and only cheese and bottles were left upon the table, the reunion went on into the night. As temperance was one of Washington's virtues, he had only one real reason for prolonging the meal, the pleasure of enjoying a conversation which took him away from his cares and afforded a relaxation from his fatigues.

General Washington received me with kindness; he mentioned the gratitude that his country would always preserve for the king and his generous assistance. He praised most highly the wisdom and skill of General comte de Rochambeau, and said that he considered it an honor to have deserved and obtained his friendship; he commended the courage and the discipline of our army; finally he had very obliging words for my father, for his long services, his many wounds, worthy adornments, said he, of a war minister. (*Editor's translation*)

Mathieu Dumas

Guillaume-Mathieu, comte de Dumas, born at Montpellier 1753, died in 1837. He came to America as an aide-de-camp to Rochambeau, served under the Revolution, emigrated in 1792, but came back after Thermidor 9; he served under Napoleon and was made a "pair de France" by Louis-Philippe. His memoirs were published as *Souvenirs du lieutenant-général comte Mathieu Dumas de 1770 à 1836*, Paris, 1839, and the same year printed in America as *Memoirs of his own time; including the Revolution, the Empire and the Restoration*. By Count Mathieu Dumas. Philadelphia, 2 vols. The extract given here is taken from vol. I, p. 30-36 of that edition. For his biography see Baron de Contenson, *op. cit.*

The whole of this comparative suspension of hostilities was well employed in putting the American army in good condition for the opening of the campaign; and general Rochambeau on his side, who was expecting the arrival of a second division, prepared himself to aid our allies with vigor. General Washington, accompanied by the marquis de la Fayette, repaired in person to the French headquarters. We had been impatient to see the hero of liberty. His dignified address, his simplicity of manners, and mild gravity, surpassed our expectation, and won every heart. After having conferred with count Rochambeau, as he was leaving us to return to his head-quarters near West Point, I received the welcome order to accompany him as far as Providence. We arrived there at night; the whole of the population had assembled from the suburbs, we were surrounded by a crowd of children carrying torches, reiterating the acclamations of the citizens; all were eager to approach the person of him whom they called their father, and pressed so closely around us that they hindered us from proceeding. General Washington was much affected, stopped a few moments, and pressing my hand, said, "We may be beaten by the English; it is the chance of war; but behold an army which they can never conquer."

I here interrupt the succinct narrative of the most remarkable events of the winter of 1781, to recall the impressions which I received during the short stay that I made in the family of the deliverer of America. The brilliant actions of great men cannot fail to be recalled by history; the anecdotes of their private life are equally worthy of being preserved because they often make us better acquainted with the principal traits of their character.

The general gave me a most cordial reception. He appeared to be highly satisfied with the dispatches which I delivered to him, in the presence of M. de la Fayette, colonel Hamilton, his aide-de-camp, and colonel Humphries, who performed the duties of chief of the staff. He withdrew to confer with them. Being invited to dinner, which was remarkably plain, I had leisure to admire the perfect harmony of his noble and fine countenance, with the simplicity of his language and the justice and depth of his observations. He generally sat long at table, and animated the conversation by unaffected cheerfulness. Much was said of the treachery of Arnold, of the firmness and moderation with which the general had just suppressed the insubordination of the troops of the state of Pennsylvania and lastly of the situation of Virginia, of the marches and counter-marches of lord Cornwallis. I was particularly struck with the marks of affection which the general showed to his pupil, his adopted son the marquis de la Fayette. Seated opposite to him, he looked at him with pleasure, and listened to him with manifest interest. One of the company, (if I remember rightly, it was, I think, colonel Hamilton, who was afterwards so unfortunately and so prematurely snatched from the hopes of his country,) related the manner in which the general had received a despatch from Sir Henry Clinton, addressed to Mr. Washington. Taking it from the hands of the flag of truce, and seeing the direction, "This letter," said he, "is directed to a planter of the state of Virginia. I shall have it delivered to him, after the end of the war; till that time it shall not be opened." A second despatch was addressed to His Excellency General Washington.

On the following day general Washington was to go to West Point, and allowed me to accompany him. Count de Charlus, who had just arrived to pay his respects to the general, and to spend some days with his friend M. de la Fayette, was likewise of the party. By rather difficult paths, we passed the mountain, at the other side of which is the plateau, surrounded by steep eminences, where block houses had been built and strong batteries had been erected, to bar the course of the river by the aid of the bend, caused by the projection of this promontory. After having visited the forts and reviewed the garrison, as the day was declining, and we were going to mount our horses, the general perceived that M. de

41

la Fayette, in consequence of his old wound, was very much fatigued. "It will be better," said he, "to return by water; the tide will assist us in ascending against the stream." A boat was soon manned with good rowers, and we embarked. The cold became excessive: we had to make our way between the large flakes of ice which the river brought down. A heavy snow and the obscurity of the night soon rendered the danger more imminent; and the management of the boat, filled with water, became increasingly difficult. We coasted the rocks which lined the right bank of the Hudson, between West Point and New Windsor, at the foot of which it is impossible to land. General Washington perceiving that the master of the boat was very much alarmed, took the helm, saying, "Courage, my friends; I am going to conduct you, since it is my duty to hold the helm." After having with much difficulty made our way against the stream and the ice, we landed, and had to walk a league before we reached the headquarters.

Guillaume de Deux-Ponts

Guillaume, comte de Deux-Ponts, brother of Christian de Forbach, marquis de Deux-Ponts, came with his brother and was second in command of the Deux-Ponts regiment. His memoirs were never published in France. They appeared in America as *My Campaigns in America: A Journal kept by Count William de Deux Ponts, 1780-1781*. Translated from the French manuscript by Samuel Abbott Green. Boston, 1868. Pages 126 and 127 are reproduced here. For his biography see the introduction of Green and Baron de Contenson, *op. cit.*

WASHINGTON HEARS OF THE ARRIVAL
OF THE FRENCH ARMY

On the 5th of September (1781), we encamped at Chester, where we learned the authentic news of the arrival of the Count de Grasse with twenty-eight ships of the line, and three thousand five hundred troops under the Marquis de St. Simon, who landed them on the 27th of August, the day after his arrival, with orders to join the corps of the Marquis de Lafayette.

The joy which this welcome news produced among all troops, which penetrates General Washington and the Count de Rochambeau, is more easy to feel than to express.

I have been equally surprised and touched at the true and pure joy of General Washington. Of a natural coldness and of a serious and noble approach, which in him is only true dignity, and which adorns so well the chief of a whole nation, his features, his physiognomy, his deportment—all were changed in an instant. He put aside his character as arbiter of North America and contented himself for the moment with that of a citizen, happy at the good fortune of his country. A child, whose every wish had been gratified, would not have experienced a sensation more lively, and I believe that I am doing honor to the feelings of this rare man, in endeavoring to express all their ardor.

Chastellux

François-Jean, chevalier and later marquis de Chastellux, born in 1734, was a philosopher, a poet and a soldier; he served as major general in Rochambeau's army and died in 1788. His biography has been recently written by Miss Fanny Varnum: *Un philosophe cosmopolite au XVIII° siècle,* Paris 1936. His memoirs appeared as *Voyages dans l'Amérique Septentrionale dans les années 1780, 1781, 1782.* Paris, 2 vols, 1786; the following year appeared the *Travels in North America, in the years 1780, 1781, 1782. By the Marquis de Chatellux . . . translated from the French by an English gentleman who resided in America during that period. With notes by the translator.* Dublin, 2 vols, 1787. The abstracts given here are taken from that edition. They are undoubtedly to be counted among the most important documents concerning Washington.

CHASTELLUX MEETS HIS EXCELLENCY
AND HIS "FAMILY"

At length, after riding two miles along the right flank of the army, and after passing thick woods on the right, I found myself in a small plain, where I saw a handsome farm; a small camp which seemed to cover it, a large tent extended in the court, and several waggons round it, convinced me that this was his *Excellency's* quarter; for it is thus Mr. Washington is called in the army, and throughout America. M. de la Fayette was in conversation with a tall man, five foot nine inches high, (about five foot ten inches and a half English) of a noble and mild countenance. It was the General himself. I was soon off horseback, and near him. The compliments were short; the sentiments with which I was animated, and the good wishes he testified for me were not equivocal. He conducted me to his house, where I found the company still at table, although the dinner had been long over. He presented me to the Generals Knox, Waine, Howe, &c. and to his *family,* then composed of Colonels Hamilton and Tilgman, his Secretaries and his Aides de Camp, and of Major Gibbs, commander of his guards; for in England and America, the Aides de Camp, Adjutants and other officers attached to the General, form what is called his *family.* A fresh dinner was prepared for me and mine; and the present was prolonged to keep me company. A few glasses of claret and madeira accelerated the acquaintances I had to make, and I soon felt myself at my ease near the greatest and the best of men. The goodness and benevolence which characterize him, are evident from every thing about him; but the confidence he gives birth to never occasions improper familiarity; for the sentiment he inspires has the same origin in every individual, a profound esteem for his virtues, and a high opinion of his talents.* About nine o'clock the general officers

* Rochefoucault has said, "That no man is a hero to his Valet de Chambre." Without combating the general justice of the remark, this excellent man is most certainly an exception. Those who are the nearest to his person love him the most, but this is never separated from a

withdrew to their quarters, which were all at a considerable distance; but as the General wished me to stay in his own house, I remained some time with him, after which he con-

marked degree of respect and admiration. This is not only the universal testimony, but I had myself the high gratification of observing it. Before the war, there was not a gentleman within the circle of his neighbourhood, who, having important concerns, or a family to leave behind him, did not close his eyes in peace, could he be so fortunate as to get Mr. Washington for an executor: an unequivocal proof of his integrity. I have likewise the strongest testimony to refute those injurious insinuations which have been propagated by envy, ignorance, or party malevolence, with the view of depreciating his talents. I had particular business to transact with him in 1782, respecting the estates of an old friend to whom he was executor, but which from peculiar circumstances had been totally neglected by the noble heirs in England, from the year 1771, indeed I may say, from the year 1767. I found his Excellency in winter quarters at Philadelphia; on entering into conversation on the subject, which was of *a most complicated nature,* the General modestly apprized me, that from the active and turbulent situation in which he had long been placed, never having been at his own house in Virginia since the year 1775, but one night on his return from York Town, he was ignorant of his own affairs, and was consequently afraid he could afford me but little information respecting those in question: but what was my astonishment, when, after this prelude, he entered into an accurate detail of every thing respecting them, scarcely omitting, as I afterwards found upon the spot, the most minute particular! On my arrival in Virginia, I had an opportunity of perusing, amongst the papers, many of his letters written whilst in the active management of the affairs, which furnished me with unquestionable proofs of the clearness of his head, the honour and disinterestedness of his heart, and the uncommon perspicuity and elegance of his style; so as to convince me of the identity of the pen that produced those admirable epistolary performances, which did him so much honour during the war, and will ever mark the energy of his mind, and the excellence of his understanding. I have dwelt with the more satisfaction on this particular, as Envy, unable to detract from their merit, has made frequent attempts to rob his fame of the honour of having ever produced them; and what relates to the public opinion concerning himself he always leaves to the determination of others. This heartfelt, but faithful tribute to transcendent virtue and abilities, is the effusion of a mind unaccustomed to flattery, and in an instance where flattery neither has, *nor can have any object.* I had long revered his character before I saw him, and we all know that too much prepossession is generally unfavorable on a nearer view; but to know *him,* establishes and heightens the most favourable ideas; and I saw, and knew this truly great man, only to root in my mind the most sincere attachment, affection and veneration for his person and character.

Translator.

ducted me to the chamber prepared for my Aides de Camp and me. This chamber occupied the fourth part of his lodgings; he apologized to me for the little room he had in his disposal, but always with a noble politeness, which was neither complimentary nor troublesome.

At nine the next morning they informed me that his Excellency was come down into the parlour. This room served at once as audience chamber, and dining-room. I immediately went to wait on him, and found breakfast prepared. *Lord Stirling* had come to breakfast with us. He is one of the oldest Major-Generals in the army; his birth, his titles and pretty extensive property have given him more importance in America, than his talents could ever have acquired him. The title of *Lord,* which was refused him in England, is not here contested with him: he claimed this title from inheritance, and went to Europe to support his pretensions, but without success. A part of his estate has been dissipated by the war, and by his taste for expence; he is accused of liking the table and the bottle, full as much as becomes a Lord, but more than becomes a General. He is brave, but without capacity, and has not been fortunate in the different commands with which he has been entrusted. He was made prisoner at the affair of Long Island. In June 1777, he got into a scrape at Elizabeth Town, whilst General Washington made head against 20,000 English on the heights of Middlebrook; he there lost two or three hundred men, and three pieces of cannon: at Brandywine he commanded the right of the army, or rather the body of troops defeated by *Cornwallis*; but on all these occasions he displayed great personal courage and firmness. I conversed a long time with him, and found him to be a sensible man, not ill informed of the affairs of his country. He is old and rather dull; but with all this, he will continue to serve, because the employment, though not lucrative, helps to repair a little the disorder in his affairs; and not having quitted the service since the beginning of the war, he has, at least zeal and seniority in his favour; thus he will retain the command of the first line, to which his rank entitles

46

him; but care will be taken not to employ him on particular expeditions.*

Whilst we were at breakfast, horses were brought, and General Washington gave orders for the army to get under arms at the head of the camp. The weather was very bad, and it had already begun raining; we waited half an hour; but the General seeing that it was more likely to increase than to diminish, determined to get on horseback. Two horses were brought him, which were a present from the State of Virginia; he mounted one himself, and gave me the other. Mr. Lynch and Mr. de Montesquieu, had each of them, also, a very handsome blood horse, such as we could not find at Newport for any money. We repaired to the artillery camp, where *General Knox* received us; the artillery was numerous, and the gunners, in very fine order, were formed in parade, in the foreign manner, that is, each gunner at his battery and ready to fire. The General was so good as to apologize to me for the cannon not firing to salute me; he said, that having put all the troops on the other side of the river in motion, and apprized them that he might himself march along the right bank, he was afraid of giving the alarm, and of deceiving the detachments that were out. We gained, at length, the right of the army, where we saw the Pennsylvania line; it was composed of two brigades, each forming three battalions, without reckoning the light infantry, which were detached with the Marquis de la Fayette. General Waine, who commanded it, was on horseback, as well as the Brigadiers and Colonels. They were all well mounted: the officers also had a very military air; they were well ranged, and saluted very gracefully. Each brigade had a band of music; the march they were then playing was the *Huron.* I knew that this line, though in want of many things, was the best clothed in the army; so that his Excellency asking me whether I would proceed, and see the whole army, or go by the shortest road to the camp of the *Marquis,* I accepted the latter proposal. The troops ought to thank me

* Lord Stirling died before the end of the war.

for it, for the rain was falling with redoubled force; they were dismissed, therefore, and we arrived heartily wet at the Marquis de la Fayette's quarters, where I warmed myself with great pleasure, partaking from time to time, of a large bowl of grog, which is stationary on his table, and is presented to every officer who enters. The rain appearing to cease, or inclined to cease for a moment, we availed ourselves of the opportunity to follow his Excellency to the camp of the Marquis: we found all his troops in order of battle on the heights to the left, and himself at their head; expressing, by his air and countenance, that he was happier in receiving me there, than at his estate in Auvergne. The confidence and attachment of the troops, are for him invaluable possessions, well acquired riches, of which nobody can deprive him; but what, in my opinion, is still more flattering for a young man of his age, is the influence, the consideration he has acquired amongst the political, as well as the military order: I do not fear contradiction when I say, that private letters from him have frequently produced more effect on some states than the strongest exhortations of the Congress. On seeing him, one is at a loss which most to admire, that so young a man as he should have given such eminent proofs of talents, or that a man so tried, should give hopes of so long a career of glory. Fortunate his country, if she knows how to avail herself of them; more fortunate still should she stand in no need of calling them into exertion.

I distinguished, with pleasure, among the colonels, who were extremely well mounted, and who saluted with great grace, *M. de Gimat,* a French officer, over whom I claim the rights of a sort of military paternity, having brought him up in my regiment from his earliest youth.* This whole van-

* M. de Gimat made the following campaign at the head of a battalion of light infantry, always under the command of M. de la Fayette. At the siege of York, he attacked and carried jointly with Colonel Hamilton, the enemy's redoubt on their left. This attack was made at the same time with that of the Baron de Viomenil, on the right redoubt, and with the same success. Mr. Gimat was wounded in the foot: on his return to Europe, he was made Colonel of the regiment of Martinico.

guard consisted of six battalions, forming two brigades; but there was only one piquet of dragoons or light cavalry, the remainder having marched to the southward with *Colonel Lee*. These dragoons are perfectly well mounted, and do not fear meeting the English dragoons, over whom they have gained several advantages;* but they have never been numerous enough to form a solid and permanent body. The piquet that was kept with the army, served then as an escort to the provost Marshal, and performed the functions of the *Marechaussée,* until the establishment of a regular one, which was intended.

The rain spared us no more at the camp of the Marquis than at that of the main army; so that our review being finished, I saw with pleasure General Washington set off in a gallop to regain his quarters. We reached them as soon as the badness of the roads would permit us. At our return we found a good dinner ready, and about twenty guests, among whom were Generals Howe and Sinclair. The repast was in the English fashion, consisting of eight or ten large dishes of butcher's meat, and poultry, with vegetables of several sorts, followed by a second course of pastry, comprized under the two denominations of pies and puddings. After this the cloth was taken off, and apples and a great quantity of nuts were served, which General Washington usually continues eating for two hours, *toasting* and conversing all the time. These nuts are small and dry, and have so hard a shell, (hickory nuts) that they can only be broken by the hammer; they are served half open, and the company are never done picking and eating them. The conversation was calm and agreeable; his Excellency was pleased to enter with me into the particulars of some of the principal operations of the war, but always with a modesty and conciseness which proved that it was

---

* The *heroic* Tarleton has experienced that there is some difference between these dragoons and a surprised party of ill-armed infantry and peasants. This gentleman's forte was in the latter species of war; a forced march, a surprize, and a bloody gazette, are the records of his glory.

Translator.

from pure complaisance that he mentioned it. About half past seven we rose from table, and immediately the servants came to shorten it, and convert it into a round one; for at dinner it was placed diagonally to give more room. I was surprised at this manœuvre, and asked the reason of it; I was told they were going to lay the cloth for supper. In half an hour I retired to my chamber, fearing lest the General might have business, and that he remained in company only on my account; but at the end of another half hour, I was informed that his Excellency expected me at supper. I returned to the dining-room, protesting against this supper; but the General told me he was accustomed to take something in the evening; that if I would be seated, I should only eat some fruit, and assist in the conversation. I desired nothing better, for there were then no strangers, and nobody remained but the General's family. The supper was composed of three or four light dishes, some fruits, and above all a great abundance of nuts, which were as well received in the evening as at dinner. The cloth being soon removed, a few bottles of good claret and madeira were placed on the table.* Every sensible man

* On my return from the southward in 1782, I spent a day or two at the American camp at Verplanks Point on the North River, and had the honour of dining with General Washington. I had suffered severely from an ague, which I could not get quit of, though I had taken the exercise of a hard trotting horse, and got thus far to the northward, in the month of October. The General observing it, told me he was sure I had not met with a good glass of wine for some time, an article then very rare, but that my disorder must be frightened away; he made me drink three or four of his silver camp cups of excellent madeira at noon, and recommended to me to take a generous glass of claret after dinner, a prescription by no means repugnant to my feelings, and which I most religiously followed. I mounted my horse next morning, and continued my journey to Massachusetts, without ever experiencing the slightest return of my disorder. The American camp here, presented the most beautiful and picturesque appearance: it extended along the plain, on the neck of land formed by the winding of the Hudson, and had a view of this river to the south; behind it, the lofty mountains, covered with wood, formed the most sublime back-ground that painting can express. In the front of the tents was a regular continued portico, formed by the boughs of trees in verdure, decorated with much taste and fancy; and each officer's tent was distinguished by superior ornaments. Opposite the camp, and on distinct eminences, stood the tents of

will be of my opinion, that being a French officer, under the orders of General Washington, and what is more a good whig, I could not refuse a glass of wine offered me by him; but I confess, that I had little merit in this complaisance, and that, less accustomed to drink than any body, I accommodate myself very well to the English mode of *toasting*: you have very small glasses, you pour out yourself the quantity of wine you chuse, without being pressed to take more, and the toast is only a sort of check in the conversation, to remind each individual that he forms part of the company, and that the whole form only one society. I observed that there was more solemnity in the toasts at dinner: there were several ceremonious ones; the others were suggested by the General, and given out by his Aides de Camp, who performed the honours of the table at dinner; for one of them is every day seated at the bottom of the table, near the General, to serve the company and distribute the bottles. The toasts in the evening were given by Colonel Hamilton, without order or ceremony. After supper the guests are generally desired to give a *sentiment*; that is to say, a lady to whom they are attached by some sentiment, either of love, or friendship, or perhaps from preference only.* This supper or conversation, commonly lasted from nine to eleven, always free, and always agreeable.

The weather was so bad on the 25th, that it was impossible to me to stir, even to wait on the Generals, to whom M. de la Fayette was to conduct me. I easily consoled myself for this, finding it a great luxury to pass a whole day with General

some of the general officers, over which towered, predominant that of General Washington. I had seen all the camps in England, from many of which, drawings and engravings have been taken; but this was truly a subject worthy the pencil of the first artist. The French camp, during their stay at Baltimore, was decorated in the same style. At the camp at Verplanks, we distinctly heard the morning and evening gun of the British at Kingsbridge.

Translator.

* The English reader will see that the Author makes a small mistake here; it being the custom in America, as in England, to give a lady, *or* a sentiment, or both.

Translator.

Washington, as if he were at his house in the country, and had nothing to do. The Generals *Glover, Huntingdon,* and some others, dined with us, and the Colonels Stewart and Butler, two officers distinguished in the army. The intelligence received this day occasioned the proposed attack on Staten Island to be laid aside. The foraging party under General Starke had met with the most complete success; the enemy not having thought proper to disturb them, so that they had not stripped the posts in the quarter where it was intended to attack them; besides, that this expedition could only have been a *coup de main,* rendered very difficult by the badness of the roads from the excessive rains. It was determined therefore that the army should march the next day to winter quarters, and that I should continue my route to Philadelphia.

The weather being fair, on the 26th, I got on horseback, after breakfasting with the General. He was so attentive as to give me the horse he rode on, the day of my arrival, which I had greatly commended: I found him as good as he is handsome; but above all, perfectly well broke, and well trained, having a good mouth, easy in hand, and stopping short in a gallop without bearing the bit. I mention these minute particulars, because it is the General himself who breaks all his own horses; and he is a very excellent and bold horseman, leaping the highest fences, and going extremely quick, without standing upon his stirrups, bearing on the bridle, or letting his horse run wild; circumstances which our young men look upon as so essential a part of English horsemanship, that they would rather break a leg or an arm than renounce them.

My first visit was to General Waine, where Mr. de la Fayette was waiting to conduct me to the other general officers of the line. We were received by General Huntingdon, who appeared rather young for the rank of Brigadier-General, which he has held two years: his carriage is cold and reserved, but one is not long in perceiving him to be a man of sense and information; by General Glover, about five and forty, a little man, but active and a good soldier; by General Howe, who is one of the oldest Majors General, and who enjoys the consideration due to his rank, though from unfavourable circumstances, he has not been fortunate in war, particularly in Georgia, where he commanded with a very small force, at the time General Prevost took possession of it; he is fond of music, the arts, and pleasure, and has a cultivated mind. I remained a considerable time with him, and saw a very curious *lusus naturae,* but as hideous as possible. It was a young man of a Dutch family, whose head was become so enormous, that it took the whole nourishment from his body; and his hands and arms were so weak that he was unable to make use of them. He lies constantly in bed, with his monstrous head supported by a pillow; and as he has long been accustomed to lie on his right side, his right arm is in a state of atrophy: he is not quite an idiot, but he could never learn any thing, and has no more reason than a child of five or six years old, though he is seven and twenty. This extraordinary derangement of the animal œconomy proceeds from a dropsy, with which he was attacked in his infancy, and which displaced the bones that form the cranium. We know that these bones are joined together by sutures, which are soft in the first period of life, and harden and ossify with age. Such an exuberance, so great an afflux of humour in that, which of all the viscera seems to require the most exact proportion, as well in what relates to the life as to the understanding of man, afford stronger proof of the necessity of an equilibrium between the solids and fluids, than the existence of the final causes.

General Knox, whom we had met, and who accompanied us, brought us back to head quarters, through a wood, as the shortest way, and to fall into a road leading to his house, where we wished to pay our compliments to Mrs. Knox. We found her settled in a little farm, where she had passed part of the campaign; for she never quits her husband. A child of six months, and a little girl of three years old, formed a real *family* for the General. As for himself he is between thirty and forty, very fat, but very active, and of a gay and amiable character. Previous to the war he was a bookseller at Boston,

53

and used to amuse himself in reading some military books in his shop. Such was the origin and the first knowledge he acquired of the art of war, and the taste he has had ever since for the profession of arms. From the very first campaign, he was entrusted with the command of the artillery, and it has turned out that it could not have been placed in better hands. It was he whom M. du Coudray endeavoured to supplant, and who had no difficulty in removing him. It was fortunate for Mr. du Coudray, perhaps, that he was drowned in the *Schuylkill,* rather than to be swallowed up in the intrigues he was engaged in, and which might have been productive of much mischief.*

* General Knox who retained until the peace the same situation in the American army, commanded their artillery at the siege of York. One cannot too much admire the intelligence and activity with which he collected from all quarters, transported, disembarked and conveyed to the batteries the train destined for the siege, and which consisted of more than thirty pieces of cannon and mortars of a large bore: this artillery was extremely well served, General Knox never caring to direct it, and frequently taking the trouble himself of pointing the mortars. He scarcely ever quitted the batteries; and when the town surrendered, he stood in need of the same activity and the same resources to remove and transport the enemy's artillery, which consisted of upwards of two hundred *bouches à feu,* with all the ammunition belonging to them. The rank of Major General was the recompence of his services.

It may be observed, that if on this occasion the English were astonished at the justness of the firing, and terrible execution of the French artillery, we were not less so at the extraordinary progress of the American artillery, as well as the capacity and knowledge of a great number of the officers employed in it.

As for General Knox, to praise his military talents only, would be to deprive him of half of the eulogium which he merits: A man of understanding, a well formed man, gay, sincere and honest; it is impossible to know without esteeming him, or to see without loving him. In the text, it is said that he was a bookseller at Boston before the war; this is not perfectly the truth. He carried on trade in various articles, and according to the American custom, he sold them wholesale and retail. Books, but particularly French books, made part of this commerce, but he employed himself more in reading than selling them. Before the revolution he was one of the principal citizens of Boston; at present, he belongs to the whole world by his reputation and his success. Thus have the English, contrary to their intention, added to the ornament of the human species, by awakening talents and virtues where they thought to find nothing but ignorance and weakness.

54

On our return to head quarters, we found several General Officers and Colonels, with whom we dined. I had an opportunity of conversing more particularly with *General Waine*; he has served more than any officer of the American army, and his services have been more distinguished,* though he is yet but young. He is sensible, and his conversation is agreeable and animated.—The affair of Stoney Point has gained him much honour in the army; however, he is only a Brigadier General! This arises from the nomination to the superior ranks being vested in the states to whom the troops belong, and that the state of Pennsylvania has not thought proper to make any promotion apparently from principles of oeconomy. The remainder of the day I dedicated to the enjoyment of General Washington's company, whom I was to quit the next day. He was so good as to point out to me himself my journey, to send on before to prepare me lodgings, and to give me a Colonel to conduct me as far as Trenton. The next morning all the General's baggage was packed up, which did not hinder us from breakfasting, before we parted, he for his winter quarters, and I for my journey to Philadelphia.

Here would be the proper place to give the portrait of General Washington: but what can my testimony add to the idea already formed of him? The continent of North America, from Boston to Charles Town, is a great volume, every page of which presents his eulogium. I know, that having had the opportunity of a near inspection, and of closely observing him, some more particular details may be expected from me; but the strongest characteristic of this respectable man is the perfect union which reigns between the physical and moral qualities which compose the individual, one alone will enable you to judge of all the rest. If you are presented with medals of Caesar, of Trajan, or Alexander, on examining their fea-

---

* This might in some respect be true at the time the Marquis speaks of, but let the southern campaigns be attended to, and justice will be done to the active zeal, the wonderful exertions, the unabating courage of that great officer *General Green*; other exceptions might be made, but this stands conspicuous.

Translator.

tures, you will still be led to ask what was their stature, and the form of their persons; but if you discover, in a heap of ruins, the head or the limb of an antique *Apollo,* be not curious about the other parts, but rest assured that they all were conformable to those of a God. Let not this comparison be attributed to enthusiasm! It is not my intention to exaggerate, I wish only to express the impression General Washington has left on my mind; the idea of a perfect whole, that cannot be the produce of enthusiasm, which rather would reject it, since the effect of proportion is to diminish the idea of greatness. Brave without temerity, laborious without ambition, generous without prodigality, noble without pride, virtuous without severity; he seems always to have confined himself within those limits, where the virtues, by cloathing themselves in more lively, but more changeable and doubtful colours, may be mistaken for faults. *This is the seventh year that he has commanded the army, and that he has obeyed the Congress; more need not be said, especially in America, where they know how to appreciate all the merit contained in this simple fact.* Let it be repeated that Condé was intrepid, Turenne prudent, Eugene adroit, Catinat disinterested. It is not thus that Washington will be characterised. It will be said of him, AT THE END OF A LONG CIVIL WAR, HE HAD NOTHING WITH WHICH HE COULD REPROACH HIMSELF. If any thing can be more marvellous than such a character, it is the unanimity of the public suffrages in his favour. Soldier, magistrate, people, all love and admire him; all speak of him in terms of tenderness and veneration. Does there then exist a virtue capable of refraining the injustice of mankind; or are glory and happiness too recently established in America, for Envy to have deigned to pass the seas?

In speaking of this perfect whole of which General Washington furnishes the idea, I have not excluded exterior form. His stature is noble and lofty, he is well made, and exactly proportioned; his physiognomy mild and agreeable, but such as to render it impossible to speak particularly of any of his features, so that in quitting him, you have only the recollection of a fine face. He has neither a grave nor a familiar air, his brow is sometimes marked with thought, but never with inquietude; in inspiring respect, he inspires confidence, and his smile is always the smile of benevolence.*

But above all, it is in the midst of his General Officers, that it is interesting to behold him. General in a republic, he has not the imposing stateliness of a Marechal de France who gives *the order;* a hero in a republic, he excites another sort of respect, which seems to spring from the sole idea, that the safety of each individual is attached to his person. As for the rest, I must observe on this occasion, that the General Officers of the American army have a very military and a very becoming carriage; that even all the officers, whose characters were brought into public view, unite much politeness to a great deal of capacity; that the head quarters of this army, in short, neither presented the image of want nor inexperience. When one sees the battalion of the General's guards encamped within the precincts of his house; nine waggons, destined to carry his baggage, ranged in his court; a great number of grooms taking care of very fine horses belonging to the General Officers and their Aides de Camp; when one observes the perfect order that reigns within these precincts, where the guards are exactly stationed, and where the drums beat an alarm, and a particular retreat, one is tempted to apply to the Americans what Pyrrhus said of the Romans: *Truly these people have nothing barbarous in their discipline!* (*Travels,* vol. I, p. 112-141)

* It is impossible for any man who has had the happiness to approach the General, not to admire the accuracy of this description, and the justness and happiness with which it is developed, or to read it without the strongest emotion. It is here above all, the Translator must apologize for his author; it is not possible to do justice to the original, to feel all its elegance, it must be read in the language in which it was written. Posterity, future historians, will be grateful to the Marquis de Chastellux for this exquisite portrait; every feature, and every trait of which will stand the test of the severest scrutiny, and be handed down to distant ages in never fading colours.

Translator.

AN "INTIMATE" INTERVIEW

At the beginning of the night, I arrived at the house of Mr. *Smith,* who formerly kept an inn, though at present he lodges only his friends; but as I had not the honour to be of that number, I was obliged to go a little further, to *Hern's Tavern,* a very indifferent house, where I supped and slept. I left it the 19th, as early as possible; having still twelve miles to New-Windsor, and intending to stay only one night, I was anxious to pass at least the greatest part of the day with General Washington. I met him two miles from New-Windsor; he was in his carriage with Mrs. Washington, going on a visit to Mrs. Knox, whose quarters were a mile farther on, near the artillery barracks. They wished to return with me, but I begged them to continue their way. The General gave me one of his Aide de Camp's (Colonel *Humphreys*)* to conduct me to his house, assuring me that he should not be long in joining me, and he returned accordingly in half an hour. I saw him again with the same pleasure, but with a different sentiment from what he had inspired me with at our first interview. I felt that internal satisfaction in which self-love has some share, but which we always experience in finding ourselves in an intimacy already formed, in real society with a man we have long admired without being able to approach him. It then seems as if this great man more peculiarly belongs to us, than to the rest of mankind; hereto-

* He is at present Secretary of the Embassy to the court of France. This brave and excellent soldier is at the same time a poet of great talents: he is the author of a poem addressed to the American army, a work recently known in England, where, in spite of the national jealousy, and the affectation of depreciating every thing American, it has had such success, as to have been several times publicly read in the manner of the ancients.——(The Marquis de Chastellux may be assured that it is not by that part of the English nation who are "jealous of America, and who affect to depreciate every thing American," that the poem of Colonel Humphreys is admired; it is by that numerous and enlightened class of free spirits, who have always supported and wished prosperity to the glorious struggle of America, who rejoiced at her success, and who look forward with hope and pleasure to her rising greatness.

Translator.)

58

fore we desired to see him; henceforth, so to speak, we exhibit him; we knew him, we are better acquainted with him than others, have the same advantage over them, that a man having read a book through, has in conversation over him who is only at the beginning.

The General insisted on my lodging with him, though his house was much less than that he had at *Prakness.* Several officers, whom I had not seen at the army, came to dine with us. The principal of whom were Colonel *Malcomb,* a native of Scotland, but settled in America, where he has served with distinction in the continental army; he has since retired to his estate, and is now only a militia Colonel; Colonel Smith,* an officer highly spoken of, and who commanded a battalion of light infantry under M. de la Fayette; Colonel *Humphreys,* the General's Aide de Camp, and several others whose names I have forgot, but who had all the best *ton,* and the easiest deportment. The dinner was excellent; tea succeeded dinner, and conversation succeeded tea, and lasted till supper. The war was frequently the subject: On asking the General which of our professional books he read with the most pleasure; he told me, the King of Prussia's Instructions to

* The author having since been very intimate with Colonel Smith, can take upon himself to assert, that this young man is not only a very good soldier, but an excellent scholar. The manner of his entering into the service merits relation: he was designed for the profession of the law, and was finishing his studies at New-York, when the American army assembled there after the unfortunate affair of Long-Island. He immediately resolved to take arms in defence of his country, but his parents disapproving of this step, he enlisted as a common soldier, without making himself known, or pretending to any superior rank. Being one day on duty at the door of a General Officer, he was discovered by a friend of his family, who spoke of him to that General Officer. He was immediately invited to dinner; but he answered that he could not quit his duty; his corporal was sent for to relieve him, and he returned to his post after dinner. A few days only elapsed before that General Officer, charmed with his zeal, made him his Aide de Camp. In 1780, he commanded a battalion of light infantry, and the year following was made Aide de Camp to General Washington, with whom he remained until the peace.—(He is now Secretary to the Embassy to the court of Great Britain, and has lately married the daughter of his Excellency John Adams, Minister Plenipotentiary to that court.

Translator)

59

his Generals, and the Tactics of M. de Guibert; from whence I concluded that he knew as well how to select his authors as to profit by them.

I should have been very happy to accept of his pressing invitation to pass a few days with him; had I not made a solemn promise, at Philadelphia, to the Vicomte de Noailles, and his travelling companions, to arrive four-and-twenty hours after them if they stopped there, or at Albany if they went straight on. We were desirous of seeing *Stillwater* and *Saratoga,* and it would have been no easy matter for us to have acquired a just knowledge of that country had we not been together, because we reckoned upon General *Schuyler,* who could not be expected to make two journies to gratify our curiosity. I was thus far faithful to my engagement, for I arrived at New-Windsor the same day that they left Cress Point; I hoped to overtake them at Albany, and General Washington finding he could not retain me, was pleased himself to conduct me in his barge to the other side of the river. We got on shore at *Fish Kill Landing Place,* to gain the eastern road, preferred by travellers to the western. I now quitted the General, but he insisted that Colonel Smith should accompany me as far as *Poughkensie.* (*Travels,* vol. I, p. 349-354)

A PAINFUL PARTING

(December, 1782)

The 5th we set out at nine, and rode, without stopping, to Fish-kill, where we arrived at half past two, after a four-and-twenty miles journey through very bad roads. I alighted at *Boerorn's* tavern, which I knew to be the same I had been at two years before, and kept by Mrs. Egremont. The house was changed for the better, and we made a very good supper. We passed the North-river as night came on, and arrived at six o'clock at *Newburgh,* where I found Mr. and Mrs. Washington, Colonel *Tilgham,* Colonel *Humphreys,* and Major

Walker. The head quarters of Newburgh consist of a single house, neither vast nor commodious, which is built in the Dutch fashion. The largest room in it (which was the proprietor's parlour for his family, and which General Washington has converted into his dining-room) is in truth tolerably spacious, but it has seven doors, and only one window. The chimney, or rather the chimney-back, is against the wall; so that there is in fact but one vent for the smoke, and the fire is in the room itself. I found the company assembled in a small room which served by way of parlour. At nine supper was served, and when the hour of bedtime came, I found that the chamber, to which the General conducted me, was the very parlour I speak of, wherein he had made them place a camp-bed. We assembled at breakfast the next morning at ten, during which interval my bed was folded up, and my chamber became the sitting room for the whole afternoon; for American manners do not admit of a bed in the room in which company is received, especially when there are women. The smallness of the house, and the difficulty to which I saw that Mr. and Mrs. Washington had put themselves to receive me, made me apprehensive lest Mr. Rochambeau, who was to set out the day after me, by travelling as fast, might arrive on the day that I remained there. I resolved therefore to send to Fish-kill to meet him, with a request that he would stay there that night. Nor was my precaution superfluous, for my express found him already at the *landing,* where he slept, and did not join us till the next morning as I was setting out. The day I remained at head quarters was passed either at table or in conversation. General *Hand,* Adjutant General, Colonel *Reed* of New-Hampshire, and Major *Graham* dined with us. On the 7th I took leave of General Washington, nor is it difficult to imagine the pain this separation gave me; but I have too much pleasure in recollecting the real tenderness with which it affected him, not to take a pride in mentioning it. (*Travels,* vol. II, p. 298-300.)

Fersen

Hans-Axel, comte de Fersen, born in Stockholm, 1775, entered the service of the French King in 1770; he was "mestre de camp" in 1780 and accompanied Rochambeau as aide de camp. He became famous for assisting in the attempt to escape made by Louis XVI and the royal family, in 1791, and it was rumored at that time that the "beau Fersen" felt more tenderly than respectfully toward Marie-Antoinette. In 1792, he went back to Sweden, became ambassador and grand marshal of Sweden and was killed during a riot in Stockholm in 1810. Some of his papers have been published: *Le Comte de Fersen et la Cour de France. Extraits des papiers du Grand Maréchal de Suède, Comte Jean-Axel de Fersen,* publiés par son petit-neveu, le Baron R.M.de KlincKowström. Paris, 2 vols., 1877. See also *Lettres d'Axel de Fersen à son père pendant la Guerre de l'Indépendance d'Amérique.* Avec une introduction et des notes par le Comte F.U.Wrangel. Paris, 1929. We refer here to the first publication.

FERSEN MEETS THE MOST ILLUSTRIOUS MAN IN THE CENTURY

Newport, October 16,1780.

A fortnight ago, I went to Hartford, about forty leagues from here with M. de Rochambeau. We were only a party of six: the admiral, the chief of the engineers,Vicomte de Rochambeau, son of the general and two aides-de-camp of which I was one. An interview between General Washington and M. de Rochambeau took place in that town. M. de Rochambeau sent me ahead of the party to announce his arrival and I had the opportunity of seeing this man, the most illustrious, not to say unique, in our century. His face handsome and full of majesty, but at the same time kind and honest, expresses perfectly his moral qualities; he looks like a hero; he seems to be very distant, speaks little but is polite and gentlemanly. His countenance is overcast with sadness, but this becomes him perfectly and makes him even more attractive. His retinue was larger than ours: he was accompanied by the Marquis de Lafayette, General Nox (*sic*), chief of artillery, M. de Gouvion, a Frenchman, chief of the engineers, and six aides-de-camp. In addition, he had an escort of 22 dragoons, a necessary protection, as he had to go through a part of the country full of enemies. As they have no relays in this country, one has to take along one's own horses and to ride most of the time on account of the bad roads. Nevertheless everybody travelled in carriages except myself and the other aide-de-camp. (*Editor's translation*, from Vol. I, p. 43-44.)

Claude Blanchard

Claude Blanchard, born at Angers in 1742, came with Rochambeau as chief quarter-master of the army in 1780. He served under the Revolution and died at the Hôtel des Invalides in 1803. For his biography, see Baron de Contenson, *op. cit.* His diary was published in France, *Journal de Campagne, . . .* publié par Maurice de la Chenaie, Paris, 1881. Five years before had appeared in America *The Journal of Claude Blanchard, Commissary of the French Auxiliary Army sent to the United States during the American Revolution. 1780-1783.* Translated from a French manuscript. By William Duane and edited by Thomas Balch. Albany, 1876. This is the edition referred to in the following extracts.

AN INTIMATE PORTRAIT OF WASHINGTON

September 1780. On the 24th, our military and naval generals arrived. They had had an interview with General Washington, from whom they returned enchanted: an easy and noble bearing, extensive and correct views, the art of making himself beloved, these are what all who saw him observed in him. It is his merit which has defended the liberty of America, and if she enjoys it one day, it is to him alone that she will be indebted for it.

Note: I wrote this in 1780. The event has shown how right I was; it is to Mr. Washington's courage, to his love for his country and to his prudence that the Americans owe their success. He has never been inconsistent, never discouraged. Amidst success as amidst reverses, he was always calm, always the same; and his personal qualities have done more to keep soldiers in the American army and to procure partisans to the cause of liberty than the decrees of the congress." (p. 67-68.)

June 1781. I set out very early on the 26th and reached the American army. I stopped at Peeskill, a small village. I could hardly find a room in the inn, which was occupied by Mr. Pearson, one of the American generals. Peeskill is situated on the North river which is very broad; it is almost an arm of the sea, which vessels of war may ascend. In some respects it divides America into two parts, and it is upon this river that the fortifications of West Point are found, the important post which Arnold had intended to give to the English. I went to speak to General Pearson, who gave me an aide-de-camp, to conduct me to General Washington, whose quarters were at a distance of two miles. I found him sitting upon a bench at the door of the house where he lodged. I explained my mission to him and he gave me a letter for the quarter-master of Peeskill landing, to which I proceeded. These quarter masters have here, in the army, almost the same functions as we, but with more authority. I set out immediately upon the same horses, although I had more than eight leagues to travel and in the rain . . .

On the 29th, I got on horseback to see some barracks which had been occupied by an American regiment during the winter; my purpose was to establish a hospital there. On the road I met General Washington, who was going to review a part of his troops. He recognized me and invited me to dine with him at three o'clock. I repaired thither; there were twenty-five covers used by some officers of the army and a lady to whom the house belonged in which the general lodged. We dined under the tent. I was placed alongside the general. One of his aides-de-camp did the honors.

The table was served in the American style and pretty abundantly: vegetables, roast beef, lamb, chickens, salad dressed with nothing but vinegar, green peas, puddings and some pie, a kind of tart, greatly in use in England and among the Americans, all this being put upon the table at the same time. They gave us on the same plate, beef, green peas, lamb &c. At the end of the dinner the cloth was removed and some Madeira wine was brought, which was passed around, whilst drinking different healths, to the king of France, the French army, etc. I rose when I heard General Washington ask for his horses, because I desired to have a conversation with him and Mr. Coster, the purveyor of our army, who had arrived and spoke French well. We all three left the table; the other officers remained; the lady also withdrew at the same time as we. Our conference being ended, the general proposed to us to return again to the table for a moment, whilst waiting for the time of departure. Again some healths were drunk, among others that of the Count de Grasse; then everyone rose from the table. I have dwelt upon the details of this dinner, because everything that relates to General Washington seems interesting to me.

I have already described his figure. His physiognomy has something grave and serious; but it is never stern, and, on the contrary, becomes softened by the most gracious and amiable smile. He is affable and converses with his officers familiarly and gaily. I was not sufficiently accustomed to the English language to maintain a connected conversation with him; nevertheless we exchanged some words, for instance, respecting the battle of the Chesapeake, which he considered glorious to our arms. He excused himself respecting the entertainment which he had given me, to which I replied that I found myself in good case in America, better than in Corsica, where I had been for a long time. As to this subject he told me that the English papers announced that the Corsicans were about to revolt and create a diversion against us. I replied that I had no fear of it, that the Corsicans were not dangerous, and that Paoli was not Washington. In the evening I saw him again; he had come to see General Pearson, in whose house I was lodging. He invited me to come and dine with him as long as I remained in his quarters. On the next day, passing by his house again, he stopped there, caused me to be called, and proposed to me to take me to dine at the house of one of the American generals to which he was going. I thanked him, on account of some business, and he invited me in the most polite manner in the world for the next day.

July, 1781. I went thither, indeed; it was the first of July. I found the table served as the first time with about the same number of guests. I was alongside of General Washington and another general named Lord Stirling (he claimed to be an English lord). General Washington seemed, for a moment, to be somewhat absent, at other times he joined in the conversation and appeared to be interested in it. There was a clergyman at this dinner who blessed the food and said grace after they had done eating and had brought on the wine. I was told that General Washington said grace when there was no clergyman at table, as fathers of a family do in America. The first time that I dined with him there was no clergyman and I did not perceive that he made this prayer; yet I remember that, on taking his place at table, he made a gesture and said a word which I took for a piece of politeness, and which perhaps was a religious action. In this case, his prayer must have been short; the clergyman made use of more forms.

We remained a pretty long time at table. They drank twelve of fifteen healths with Madeira wine. In the course of the meal beer was served and *grum,* rum mixed with water.

On the 2d the American army left the camp of Peekskill to advance near to New York. . . . General Washington himself departed, and I saw him pass with his staff and an escort of dragoons. (P. 115, 116, 117, 118, 119.)

July 1782. On the 20th we stopped at Alexandria, a city situated upon the Potomac, where ships of fifty guns can approach. This city is perfectly well situated for becoming commercial. Therefore they have built much there; it may become considerable, still it is not much. General Washington's residence, that in which he was born, is situated between Colchester and Alexandria. Mrs Washington is a woman of about fifty years of age; she is small and fat, her appearance is respectable. She was dressed very plainly and her manners were simple in all respects; she had with her three other ladies, her relations. As to the house it is a country residence, the handsomest that I have yet seen in America, it is symmetrically built and has two stories, counting the false roofs, wherein some pretty chambers have been constructed. All rooms are furnished with taste.

There are in the places around, many huts for the negroes, of whom the general owns a large number, who are necessary to him for his large possessions, which are supposed to amount to ten thousand acres of land. (The acre is very nearly of the same extent as our arpent.) Among these some of good quality is found, and I have observed some of it of this sort. A large part is woodland, where Mr. Washington, before the war, enjoyed the pleasure of the chase, which had inclined him to the military life he has since led. The environs of his house are not fertile and the trees that we see there do not appear to be large. Even the garden is barren. What decided the general's parents to choose this dwelling place is the situation which is very handsome. The Potomac flows at the foot of the garden and the largest ships of war can anchor there. It has different branches of a kind of bays and in this place is about a league broad. The whole makes a very agreeable prospect. The opposite shore needs rather more houses and villages. Taken all together, it is a handsome residence and worthy of General Washington. In the evening, we left her respectable company after having spent a very agreeable and truly interesting day. (P. 166-167.)

67

Abbé Robin

Little is known of the good abbé who was attached to Rochambeau's army as chaplain on Franklin's recommendation. His book, too enthusiastic and naive, was severely attacked in France when it was published. The abbé has not fared better at the hand of Mr. Bernard Faÿ, *L'Esprit révolutionnaire,* p. 120, 121. I cannot entirely share in the unreserved condemnation pronounced by his critics. Robin was a goodly soul and his relation is not entirely devoid of value. See also Frank Monaghan, *French Travellers in the United States, 1765-1932,* New York Public Library, 1933. The following extract is taken from *Nouveau Voyage dans l'Amérique Septentrionale, en l'année 1781; et Campagne de l'Armée de M. le Comte de Rochambeau.* Par M. l'Abbé Robin. A Philadelphie, et se trouve à Paris, chez Moutard. 1782.

A FRENCH ARMY CHAPLAIN SEES WASHINGTON

From the camp at Philipsburg, August 4, 1781.

I saw Washington, the man who is the soul and support of one of the greatest revolutions that has ever happened! I gazed at him earnestly with the eagerness that is always aroused by the presence of great men. It seems that one may find in their features the marks of the genius which sets them apart and places them above their fellow men. More than any other man Washington can vindicate this opinion: a tall, noble and well proportioned figure, an open, kind and calm expression, an appearance simple and modest, he strikes, he interests Frenchmen, Americans and even his enemies. At the head of a nation in which every individual shares in the supreme power and coercive legislation is still without strength, where climate, customs inspire little energy, where partisan spirit, self interest, apathy and national indolence slow down, suspend and upset the best planned measures, he knew how to impress upon his soldiers an absolute subordination, to make them eager to deserve his praise, to make them fear even his silence, to keep up their confidence even after defeats, to gain the most glorious reputation and obtain the most extensive powers without arousing envy or creating suspicion, to show himself at all time superior to chance, to discover new resources in the midst of adversity, as if his faculties had grown as difficulties increased, never to have more reserves than when they seemed to be exhausted; never more fiercely to strike the enemy than after been defeated; to stimulate the enthusiasm of the least enthusiastic of all peoples; to compel respect and recognition from men whose main interest was to deny them to him; to put his plans into effect through means which escaped the very men who were his instruments; fearless in the midst of dangers, but seeking danger only when the good of the country was at stake; choosing to temporize and to remain on the defensive because he expected everything from time and knew the temper of his country; thrifty and moderate in his own affairs and spending lavishly for the common cause, like Peter the Great he led his soldiers to victory through defeats; like Fabius, but with fewer resources and more obstacles, he conquered without fighting and saved his country. Such is the idea that one forms of this great man on seeing him, on scrutinizing the happenings in which he took part and when listening to those who are closest to him. Through all the land he appears like a benevolent god; old men, women, children they all flock eagerly to catch a glimpse of him when he travels and congratulate themselves because they have seen him. People carrying torches follow him through the cities; his arrival is marked by public illuminations; the Americans, though a cold people who even in the midst of troubles have always sought the dictates of methodical reasoning, have waxed enthusiastic about him and their first songs inspired by spontaneous sentiments have been consecrated to the glorification of Washington. (*Editor's translation.* Robin, p. 61-64.)

III.

Diplomats, Travelers and Observers

GÉRARD

BARBÉ-MARBOIS

MANDRILLON

MAZZEI

BRISSOT DE WARVILLE

MOUSTIER

TERNANT

CHATEAUBRIAND

MOREAU DE SAINT-MÉRY

PH. GUILBERT

GENET

ADET

LA ROCHEFOUCAULD-LIANCOURT

PLANE

CRÈVECŒUR

Gérard

On Alexandre Gérard, first French Minister to the United States, the latest and most authoritative work is *Dispatches and Instructions of Conrad-Alexandre Gérard, 1778-1780.* With an historical introduction and notes by John J. Meng. The Johns Hopkins Press, Baltimore, 1939. A cold, dispassionate and realistic diplomat, Gérard never indulged in sentimental effusions. He gave Washington in the two following excerpts as much praise as he could give to any man.

GÉRARD TO VERGENNES

Philadelphia, December 30, 1778.

. . . . . I had several conversations with the President of the Congress and General Washington . . . General Washington seemed to approve of my principles and my suggestions, as much as his character infinitely cold, prudent and reserved permitted to expect from him. He repeated the substance of the letter I had the honor of sending you and declared that an expedition against Canada was not practical. . . He thanked me repeatedly for my reflections and explanations; he manifested much respect and admiration for the King, an unreserved confidence in the disposition of His Majesty toward America and a great scrupulousness in his adherence to the Alliance of the States with His Majesty. Since this General has come here I have seen him every day; he seems to deserve as much praise as a man and a Citizen as for his military talents. (*Editor's translation.* Meng, p. 457-458.)

GÉRARD TO VERGENNES

Philadelphia, March 8, 1779

It is certain that if General Washington were ambitious and scheming, it would have been entirely in his power to

73

make a revolution; but nothing on the part of the General or the Army has justified the shadow of a suspicion. The General sets forth constantly this principle that one must be a Citizen first and an officer afterwards. (*Editor's translation*. Meng, p. 567).

Barbé-Marbois

François Marbois, later marquis de Barbé-Marbois, was born in Metz in 1745. He entered the diplomatic service and in June 1779 was sent to America as secretary to the Chevalier de la Luzerne who was to succeed Gérard as Minister plenipotentiary from the King of France. As consul-general and chargé d'affaires he stayed in the United States until 1785. In 1929, Professor Eugene Parker Chase, of Lafayette College, translated and edited with an introduction and notes *The Letters of François, Marquis de Barbé-Marbois, during his residence in the United States as secretary of the French legation. 1779-1785*. Duffield and Company, New York. The original manuscript remained in the hands of a descendant of Barbé-Marbois; but several parts of it, if not the whole of it, circulated in Paris and partial copies exist in the Bibliothèque de la Fondation Thiers and in the archives of the Ministry of Foreign Affairs. The part reprinted here with the kind permission of Professor Chase and of Dodd, Mead, and Company, does not appear in these copies. It is much to be regretted that the French original has never been published; the translation of Professor Chase however seems to reproduce excellently its vivacity and easy conversational tone.

LA LUZERNE ET BARBÉ-MARBOIS MEET WASHINGTON AT FISHKILL

(September 12, 1779)

In spite of all the objections of M. de la Luzerne, General Washington came to meet him at Fishkill. He received us with a noble, modest, and gentle urbanity and with that

74

graciousness which seems to be the basis of his character. He is fifty years old, well built, rather thin. He carries himself freely and with a sort of military grace. He is masculine looking, without his features' being less gentle on that account. I have never seen anyone who was more naturally and spontaneously polite. His eyes are blue and rather large, his mouth and nose are regular, and his forehead open. His uniform is exactly like that of his soldiers. Formerly, on solemn occasions, that is to say on days of battle, he wore a large blue sash, but he has given up that unrepublican distinction. I have been told that he preserves in battle the character of humanity which makes him so dear to his soldiers in camp. I have seen him for some time in the midst of his staff, and he has always appeared even-tempered, tranquil, and orderly in his occupations, and serious in his conversation. He asks few questions, listens attentively, and answers in a low tone and with few words. He is serious in business. Outside of that, he permits himself a restricted gaiety. His conversation is as simple as his habits and his appearance. He makes no pretensions, and does the honors of his house with dignity, but without pompousness or flattery. His aides-de-camp preside at his table and offer the toasts. Before being the head of the American army, he did not disdain the care of his farm. To-day, he sometimes throws and catches a ball for whole hours with his aides-de-camp. He is reverent without bigotry, and abhors swearing, which he punishes with the greatest severity. As to his public conduct, ask his compatriots, and the universe. If you like historical parallels, I might compare him to Timoleon who freed the Sicilians from the tyranny of the Carthaginians, and who joined to his military qualities those which make up an excellent citizen, and who after having rendered his country signal services lived as a private citizen, ambitious neither of power nor honors, and was satisfied to enjoy modestly the glory of having given liberty to a powerful nation.

We embarked with the General on the North River, or the Hudson, and sailed down it with the tide to West Point

75

where the headquarters are, surrounded by the chief posts of the American army. The general held the tiller, and during a little squall which required skill and practice, proved to us that this work was no less known to him than are other bits of useful knowledge. The river lies between two steep banks covered with trees. Its bed sometimes narrows to a third of a mile or widens to almost three-quarters of a league. On the right, near to West Point, the mountains go back from the river a little and allow a space of about thirty arpents where the tents of the general and the officers attached to him are placed. The divisions of the army are around this spot, on heights of which the summits are covered with forts and redoubts. The air is pure and healthful, and we saw only forty sick in the hospital.

DINNER WITH WASHINGTON

During dinner the conversation touched on the great things which the Americans had done. All the generals and the higher officers were there. It was interesting to see this meeting of these warriors, each of them a patriot renowned for some exploit, and this military meal, served in a tent in the midst of the apparatus of arms, in the heart of the former possessions of our enemies, to a French minister and officers, was to all of us a memorable novelty.

I had been seated near the general, and as he inspires confidence, after some general remarks we discussed interesting subjects fairly freely. He spoke of the fine behavior of my compatriots and of the glory which they had won in America.

Everything around us was interesting to me. The river was being driven back by the tide, and the waves came right up to the tent-pins, where they broke with a solemn roar. A few steps away from us musicians played military and tuneful French airs. The banks and the forests of the mountain answered long to the cannon shots fired to the health of the King and Queen, and the opposite bank shone with the fires which the soldiers had lighted. Before my eyes was

76

one of the most admirable spectacles in the world—the valiant
and generous leader of a brave nation fighting for liberty. I
was moved, and felt my eyes grow moist.

Tears again! Your diarist is a sad and tearful person! He
laments the departure of a merchant vessel, he weeps because
he finds himself dining in a tent with people playing French
music beside him . . . I beg you, Mademoiselle, to tell Madame
d'Inveau that I was wrong, that I ask forgiveness, and that I
promise not to do it again. But what would you? Nature has
made me in this way, and you will find that I am not the only
one.

The general told me that he was drinking the health of
the Marquis de Lafayette, and asked me if I had seen him
before my departure. I answered that I had, and added that
he spoke of him with the tenderest veneration. I said that
the conduct of M. de Lafayette in America had made him
generally esteemed, and had caused him to deserve the dis-
tinctions and favor granted him by the King. Washington
blushed like a fond father whose child is being praised. Tears
fell from his eyes, he clasped my hand, and could hardly utter
the words: "I do not know a nobler, finer soul, and I love
him as my own son."

Joseph Mandrillon

According to Mr. Bernard Faÿ, Joseph Mandrillon was a
young French merchant who made ample use of the English
travellers in various compilations on the United States, (*op.
cit.*, p. 125), although Professor Monaghan (*French travellers
in the United States,* p. 65) writes under his name "thought
to have travelled in the United States before the Revolutionary war." His *Spectateur américain, ou remarques géné-
rales sur l'Amérique Septentrionale et sur la république des
Treize Etats-Unis,* was published at Amsterdam in 1784. A
second edition was published at Amsterdam and Bruxelles in

1785. We quote here from his *Fragmens de politique et de littérature . . . offerts comme étrennes à mes amis, le 1ᵉʳ janvier 1788.* Paris et Bruxelles, 1788.

PORTRAIT OF GENERAL WASHINGTON

Oh, that I had received at birth the genius and the eloquence of the famous orators of Greece and Rome! Why can I not steal their brush for a moment in order to draw with quick strokes the portrait of the greatest man that has ever appeared in America, and one of the greatest that has ever lived! With what energy, with what enthusiasm would I not celebrate his splendid virtues! Who could be jealous of the tribute I am paying him? Who could ever tax me with being a flatterer?

We no longer live in those barbarous ages when tyrants received incense, when people would call heroes men indulging in every vice and so much feared that nobody dared to give them offense. We no longer live in those ages when cruel monarchs paid hired writers to disguise their crimes and lend them virtues. Our age, more enlightened, portrays in its history monarchs and individuals such as they were; truth characterizes it. The reverence in which General Washington is held by the public results from the most severe scrutiny of his conduct. Careful of his reputation and eager to receive the approbation of his fellow countrymen, he enjoys it without taking pride in it and without ostentation. He is fair enough to himself to believe that he deserves his fame, and he also knows that posterity which erects and overthrows statues will never overthrow the trophies raised in his honor. Only an illiterate barbarian or a savage ignorant of our history could mistake his statue for that of a tyrant and strike it with his axe. But even if from the fragments of the inscription one could save only the name of Washington, the chieftain of this savage or of this barbarian, informed by tradition of the American revolution, would punish this outrage and restore the monument; and on the pedestal one would

78

read: *Ignorance had overthrown it, justice has raised it again: Mortals, revere his memory.*

NOTE. This book was already in print, when a letter from a Philadelphia correspondent, dated August 20, informed us that the United States in Congress assembled had unanimously resolved: That an equestrian statue would be raised in honor of General Washington in the place where the seat of Congress will be established. We congratulate ourselves on having the opportunity to add this interesting note and for having thought of the same project as Congress did.

This will be a bronze statue and it will represent the general in a Roman garb, holding in his right hand the baton of commander in chief, with a laurel crown upon his head. The statue will be placed on a marble pedestal and in bas reliefs will be represented the most remarkable episodes of the war during which the General was in personal command: namely, the evacuation of Boston by the British, the capture of the Hessians at Trenton; the battle of Prince-Town; the battle of Monmouth, and the reddition of Yorktown, when Lord Cornwallis was taken prisoner. On the front of the pedestal the following inscription will be engraved:

The United States in Congress assembled ordered in the year of our Lord 1783, to erect this statue in honor *of George Washington, most illustrious commander in chief of the army of the United States of America, during the war which defended and secured their sovereignty and their independence.*

The statue will be cast in France, by the best artist in Europe, from the best likeness that can be procured of General Washington. The expense will be borne by the treasury of the United States.

While waiting for a more elegant pen to write a suitable inscription for the statue of this great man, I may be permitted to suggest a tentative form:

> Peuples de l'univers, célébrez *Washington,*
> Célébrez ses vertus, ses talens & son nom:
> Politique & guerrier, sauveur de la patrie,
> Il honora son siècle & fit taire l'envie.

It is gratifying to observe, that while enjoying a glorious peace, one of the first thoughts of these peoples is to pay their debt of gratitude by raising the first statue to be erected on the soil of the new world. As bold as Condé, as prudent as Turenne, as skillfull as Eugene, as disinterested as Catinat, Washington will make posterity acknowledge in addition that with so many brilliant qualities, he knew how to remain modest, and that at the end of a long civil war, he could reproach himself with nothing.

After being the soul and support of one of the greatest events in this century, it is only just that Washington's days should glide by cloudlessly, quietly surrounded with public honors and veneration. Occasionally, nature places the soul of a great man in a feeble body; but when one speaks of a man whose traits and stature are unknown, it is pleasant to fancy this man as having received all the gifts of nature, and it is pleasant to believe that his features bear the stamp of the genius that distinguishes him and raises him above his fellow beings.

No better example than Washington can be found to confirm this opinion. A high stature, noble and well proportioned, a quiet and kind expression, such harmonious features that nobody will ever mention any in particular and that after leaving him one remembers only a fine man, a fine face, a modest and simple countenance, a character attractive and firm without being harsh, a male courage, an uncommon penetration enabling him to grasp the whole of whatever is presented to his judgment, a consummate experience in war as well as in politics, as efficient in the council as on the battlefield, love for his country, forcing the admiration of an enemy he knew how to fight and conquer, modest in victory, great in reverses and turning them to public advantage instead of being discouraged by them. He knows how to obey as well as to command and never used his power and the obedience of his army to transgress the laws of his country or alter the orders he received. Skilled in the art of judging men, he could govern free citizens in peaceful times and through his example, his activity and his energy he was able to teach them to seek glory and to face dangers under a harsh climate and during severe winters. Soldiers eager to be praised by him feared even his silence; no general was ever better obeyed or better supported. Filled with greater ambition for his country than for himself, he never took any risk heedlessly; the only purpose of his military operations was the preservation of the country, and from his country alone he expected to obtain fame. His favorite principle always was to gain time, to remain on the defensive; without engaging the enemy in a frontal attack he managed to harass them, to wear them out through raids and sudden attacks, the opportunity of which could be seized only by a great man. Like Camillus he left the pleasures of rural life and rushed to save his country; like Fabius he saved it through temporisation; like Peter the Great he defeated the enemy by making use of the experience acquired in defeat. There is no private individual, there is no monarch even in Europe who would not covet the glory of having played as brilliant a part as Washington. It is reported that the King of Prussia when sending him a sword wrote this only address: *From the greatest general of the Old World to the greatest general of the New World.*

If ever a mortal has received during his lifetime a full measure of glory; if ever a citizen has received from his country full reward for his services and talents, it is my hero. Beloved, admired and greeted everywhere he was given by everyone heartfelt tributes of respect. When he enters a city or goes through a village, old people, women, children all accompany him with applause; all shower blessings upon him; in every heart he has a temple hallowed by respect and friendship. How I love to picture the French general (M. de Rochambeau), equally beloved and honored by his army, seated at dinner by Washington and exclaiming that he had never known either what true glory or a really great man were until he had met him. Should America devastated by terrific natural cataclysms disappear entirely, one would remember Washington as the defender of liberty, the friend of men and the avenger of an oppressed people. (*Editor's translation.* Mandrillon, ch. V, p. 165-170.)

Philip Mazzei

Filippo Mazzei, born in Florence in 1752, arrived in Virginia in 1773 and settled near Monticello. Sent by Jefferson as Virginia's agent in Europe, a man of parts and of intrigue he published in Paris, in 1788, probably on Jefferson's suggestion, his *Recherches Historiques et Politiques sur les Etats-*

Unis de l'Amérique Septentrionale . . . par un Citoyen de Virginie. Avec quatre lettres d'un Bourgeois de New Heaven [sic] *sur l'unité de la législation.* 4 vols., 1788. The main purpose was to refute and correct both abbé Mably and abbé Raynal. The "bourgeois de New Haven" was Condorcet. For his curious career which ended in Pisa in 1816, see *Philip Mazzei, friend of Jefferson. His life and letters.* By Richard Cecil Garlick. The Johns Hopkins Press, 1933.

GENERAL WASHINGTON, THE MARQUIS DE LA FAYETTE AND THE FOUNDATION OF THE SOCIETY OF THE CINCINNATI

If the institution of the Society of the Cincinnati has beclouded to some extent in Europe the character of General Washington, no American nor even any of the Europeans who were in a position to know him personally have shared these suspicions. It was said that he should have opposed this institution or at least refused to become its president; and M. le Comte de Mirabeau has accused him of vanity and cunning not to say duplicity. Such accusations are in flat contradiction with what is known of the character of a man who cannot be reproached with anything except excessive unselfishness, too much modesty and a diffidence perhaps exaggerated. A few facts will suffice to prove this point.

When General Washington accepted, after much resistance, to take command of the army, he proposed to let Congress provide for the expense of his table, declaring that he would accept no personal compensation whatsoever; he even refused to receive his share of the lands which were distributed among the former army officers according to their ranks.* Before the Revolution, he had an income large enough to provide abundantly for all the comforts of life, and to enable him to receive his friends and acquaintances in a seemly and hospitable manner. But recently it has been generally felt that

* The Marquis de la Fayette did the same. One might say that he made it a rule to follow General Washington in everything.

he might not be able to do so any longer. There is not one single officer on the whole continent who will forsake the pleasure of spending a few days with his General; there is no European traveller who does not eagerly wish to visit General Washington. The result is that his house is continuously filled with strangers who bring with them an even larger number of servants and horses; as there is no village in the vicinity and no inn within reach, the General has to take charge of everything.

At the end of the war, people felt that it would be right to provide for the increase in his expense which had been foreseen; but when the matter was brought up in Congress, the representatives who knew best the mind of the General made it clear that it was useless to discuss the matter, because of his unshakable resolution not to receive any reward.

At the beginning of 1785, the General Assembly of Virginia attempted to take measures to compensate him for it to some extent and flattered themselves that they would make him accept a present. It had been decided to open to navigation the James and Potomack rivers up to the Falls. The shares of these two companies were worth 300 dollars; the Assembly ordered the Treasurer to buy fifty of each, and requested the Governor to present them to the General as a token of the gratitude of the State which had been honored by his birth.

Before the decree of the Assembly was communicated officially to General Washington, I went to see Mr. Mason just a few days after the General had visited him. They were schoolmates, had always been close together, and Mr. Mason's opinion was always of great weight with his friend. He had attempted to prove to him that the gift intended for him by his State was in fact the repayment of a debt and only part of the debt. The reasons advanced to persuade him not to refuse were worthy of a man who combines good judgment and a great logical power; all his efforts were in vain. The General objected that he had no children; that if his income was not sufficient he would rather sell part of his lands since his relatives were in no need of his succession; that he felt an in-

83

vincible reluctance to accept anything and that he hoped that this was not vanity (*I hope it is not vanity*). Such were his very words.

My readers will not hear without some pleasure the account of another incident which shows in General Washington a mastery over his pride carried perhaps to an unprecedented degree. During the first days of the war, several citizens were dissatisfied with the tactics of the General. They compared him with Fabius Cunctator and this was not to praise him. They preferred to him General Lee, then General Gates whose reputation had been increased through his successes at the battle of Saratoga, although several subordinate officers, like Lincoln, Morgan and the traitor Arnold should have shared in his glory. The party opposed to the General was made up of men who had talents and the means to call attention to themselves; if they did not declare themselves openly it was only because public opinion held them in check. They were well known, they were working underground and none of them has ever admitted it.

After a whole year of rumors injurious to the commander in chief and which might have been detrimental to the country, Congress having ignored them for a long time, sent to Washington's camp a deputation of three members among whom was Mr. John Harvie, my friend and neighbour. The deputation realized immediately how unfounded were these popular rumors and Mr. Harvie being alone with the General: "My dear General," said he, "if you had given some explanation, all these rumors would have been silenced a long time ago."—"How could I exculpate myself without doing harm to the public cause?" answered this great man whose virtue in these circumstances seems to be beyond any praise.

Anecdotes provide the best indications for the understanding of the true character of men. It would take a whole book to gather all these sayings of General Washington proving his absolute mastery over his pride, his extreme unselfishness and his rare patriotism. I singled out the two I have just related because they might have been forgotten, and because they

84

demonstrate how necessary it is to think over everything before crediting anything which might disparage great characters.

If General Washington had believed that the Society of the Cincinnati could at any time do harm to the cause of liberty, he certainly would have attempted to prevent its establishment by sage and moderate advice in keeping with his ordinary conduct and character. (*Editor's translation*. Mazzei, Vol. IV, p. 115-121.)

Brissot

On Jean-Pierre Brissot, son of an inn keeper, who took the name of Brissot-Warville and was an ardent abolitionist, an enthusiastic apostle of the American gospel of liberty, see the vivid and rather ironical sketch of Bernard Faÿ (*op. cit.*, pp. 156-160). As far as I know there is no biography of Brissot. He related his experiences in America in his *Nouveau Voyage dans les Etats-Unis, fait en 1788;* par J. P. Brissot Paris, 3 vols. 1791. The translation appeared the following year as *New Travels in the United States of America. Performed in 1788.* New York, 1792. The following passages are taken from the American edition.

BRISSOT VISITS MOUNT VERNON (1788)

I hastened to arrive at Mount Vernon, the seat of General Washington, ten miles below Alexandria, on the same river. On this route you traverse a considerable wood, and after having passed over two hills, you discover a country house of an elegant and majestic simplicity. It is preceded by grass-plats; on one side of the avenue are the stables, on the other a green-house, and houses for a number of Negro mechanics. In a spacious back yard are turkies, geese, and other poultry. This house overlooks the Potomack, enjoys an extensive prospect, has a vast and elevated portico on the front next the river, and a convenient distribution of the apartments within.

The General came home in the evening fatigued with having been to lay out a new road in some part of his plantations. You have often heard him compared to Cincinnatus: the comparison is doubtless just. This celebrated General is nothing more at present than a good farmer, constantly occupied in the care of his farm and the improvement of cultivation. He has lately built a barn, one hundred feet in length, and considerably more in breadth, destined to receive the productions of his farm, and to shelter his cattle, horses, asses, and mules. It is built on a plan sent him by that famous English farmer, Arthur Young. But the General has much improved the plan. This building is in brick, it costs but three hundred pounds; I am sure in France it would have cost three thousand. He planted this year eleven hundred bushels of potatoes. All this is new in Virginia, where they know not the use of barns, and where they lay up no provisions for their cattle. His three hundred Negroes are distributed in different log-houses, in different parts of his plantation, which in this neighbourhood consists of ten thousand acres. Colonel Humphreys, that poet of whom I have spoken, assured me that the General possesses, in different parts of the country, more than two hundred thousand acres.

Every thing has an air of simplicity in his house; his table is good, but not ostentatious; and no deviation is seen from regularity and domestic economy. Mrs Washington superintends the whole, and joins to the qualities of an excellent house-wife, the simple dignity which ought to characterise a woman, whose husband has acted the greatest part on a theatre of human affairs; while she possesses that amenity, and manifests that attention to strangers, which render hospitality so charming. The same virtues are conspicuous in her interesting niece; but unhappily she appears not to enjoy good health.

M. de Chastellux has mingled too much of the brilliant in his portrait of General Washington. His eye bespeaks great goodness of heart, manly sense marks all his answers, and he sometimes animates in conversation, but he has no characteristic features, which renders it difficult to size him. He announces a profound discretion, and a great diffidence in himself; but at the same time, an unshaken firmness of character, when once he has made his decision. His modesty is astonishing to a Frenchman; he speaks of the American war, and of his victories, as of things in which he had no direction.

He spoke to me of M. de la Fayette with the greatest tenderness. He regarded him as his child; and foresaw, with a joy mixed with inquietude, the part that this pupil was going to act in the approaching revolution of France. He could not predict, with clearness, the event of this revolution. If, on the one side, he acknowledges the ardor and enthusiasm of the French character, on the other, he saw an astonishing veneration for their ancient government, and for those monarchs whose inviolability appeared to him a strange idea. After passing three days in the house of this celebrated man, who loaded me with kindness, and gave me much information relative to the late war, and the present situation of the United States, I returned to Alexandria. (Brissot, p. 234-236.)

LETTER XXXVI

GENERAL OBSERVATIONS ON MARYLAND AND VIRGINIA

They have much perfected in this country the English method of inoculation for the small-pox. In the manner practiced here, it is very little dangerous. General Washington assured me, that he makes it a practice to have all his Negroes inoculated, and that he never lost one in the operation. Whoever inoculates in Virginia, is obliged, by law, to give information to his neighbours within the space of two miles.

The population augments every where in these States, notwithstanding the great emigration to the Ohio. The horses of Virginia are, without contradiction, the finest in the country; but they bear double the price of those in the northern States. The practice of races, borrowed from the English by the Virginians, is falling into disuse. The places renowned for this business are all abandoned; and it is not a misfortune; they are places of gambling, drunkedness, and quarrels.

The General informed me, that he could perceive a great reformation in his countrymen in this respect; that they are less given to intoxication; that it is no longer fashionable for a man to force his guests to drink, and to make it an honour to send them home drunk; that you hear no longer the taverns resounding with those noisy parties formerly so frequent; that the sessions of the courts of justice were no longer the theatres of gambling, inebriation, and blood; and that the distinction between classes begins to disappear. (Brissot, p. 236-237.)

Moustier

On Moustier's mission as plenipotentiary from 1787 to 1790, see G. Chinard, *Trois amitiés françaises de Jefferson,* ch. II, Paris, 1927. I cannot agree here with Mr. Bernard Faÿ who, trusting probably Moustier's own dispatches, has described his mission as highly successful. The impression of the American officials was entirely different and Moustier proved himself absolutely unable to accept the American ways of living and feeling. His account of his interviews with Washington seem to indicate in the General a realistic sense of foreign politics which grew with time, and would have enabled a keener observer to forecast the policies outlined ten years later in the Farewell Address. Moustier's sister-in-law, Madame de Bréhan, accompanied him to America for reasons which did not seem quite convincing to several American officials. While visiting Washington, she made a portrait of the President which Crèvecœur used later as a frontispiece to the first volume of his *Voyage en Haute Pensylvanie.* It is reproduced here not as an artistic master piece but as a feminine and very weak interpretation of the great man. The *Correspondence of the Comte de Moustier with the Comte de*

GEORGE WASHINGTON

Né en Virginie le 11 Février 1732.

Gravé d'après le Camée peint par Madame de Bréhan à Newyork en 1789.

Montmorin,1787-1789, was published in the original French in The American Historical Review, Vol. IX, 1904.

WASHINGTON LENDS PRESTIGE TO CONGRESS
MOUSTIER TO MONTMORIN

New York, March 20, 1789.
rec. June 29.

Mylord:

A new era in the history of the United States is now being opened with the termination of Congress, first made of the Representatives of the thirteen British Colonies united in order to consult on the means of obtaining redress of their grievances against the mother country, then forming a confederacy in order to take action, and finally declaring themselves free and independent. At these different stages, Congress has never held any real authority. At the beginning, fear united the minds of men always inclined, in times of crisis and suffering, to obey the voice of a leader; the apparent deference granted to them by a General who, because of his wisdom and his luck, was looked upon as the first of the countrymen he was fighting for, and the marks of consideration given by foreign powers, contributed equally to increase considerably the prestige of Congress. (*Editor's translation.* Moustier, p. 92-93.)

WASHINGTON AS A REALIST
MOUSTIER TO MONTMORIN

New York, November 18, 1788.
rec. Feb. 11, 1789.

I have every reason to be pleased with the dispositions I found among the most influential officials of this country. My interviews with General Washington with whom I spent several days were particularly satisfactory. The result of our conversations were in his own words as follows: That most certainly the people of the United States still felt a vivid and sincere gratitude for the King and the French nation; but that self-interest alone could regulate relations between nations; that it was very easy to grant that it entirely belonged to His Majesty to see to it that the interests of the United States be closely connected with His own.

This conclusion is the more worthy of remark, as General Washington will become President of the United States if he so wishes, and that his power and influence in that capacity will be of utmost importance under the terms of the new Constitution. I endeavored, in all circumstances, without committing myself, to convey the impression that if our relations with the Americans have not heretofore been closer, the responsibility must fall upon their faulty Constitution, and that the revolution it has just undergone has always been considered as desirable by His Majesty and His council. This way of speaking seems to me useful and even necessary, if we consider that the thing is in a way accomplished and that the only course left is to make the most of it. (*Editor's translation*. Moustier, p. 92-93.)

Ternant

Chevalier Jean de Ternant born at Damvillers (Meuse), in 1751, had presented himself as volunteer to Washington, in 1778, and served as second to baron de Steuben as army inspector. He reintered the service of the King after 1783 and was sent to America as Minister plenipotentiary in March 1791. A sketch of his life is given by Commandant Lasseray, op. cit. vol. II, p. 433-436. His letters show clearly that Washington maintained a strict separation between the business of the State and his personal feelings. His dispatches are found in Frederick J. Turner, *Correspondence of the French Ministers to the United States, 1791-1797*. Annual report of the American Historical Association for the year 1903. Washington, 1904, vol. II.

Philadelphia, August 13, 1791.

SIR:

. . . On informing of my arrival the Secretary of State, Mr. Jefferson, I hastened to express my desire to see as soon as possible General Washington, as an old acquaintance, before being introduced to him in an official capacity. The same day, I was informed that the President would be delighted to see me at my earliest convenience. Our interview was very simple and marked with every sign of the most cordial and gratifying friendship. "You and I are old friends," he said at the beginning, "and it is a great pleasure to me and Mrs Washington to see you again among us." The interview lasted fully half an hour and did not touch at any moment on the object of my mission. Keeping in mind the decree of the 2nd of June last, I thought I had no right to be the first to mention it.

The following day, I announced officially my arrival, and I asked when I could present my credentials and what forms would have to be observed on this occasion. The Secretary of State, after inquiring from the President who, according to the new federal constitution "shall receive ambassadors and other public ministers," answered that the presentation of credentials would henceforth take place without any display or ceremonial and even without any speech whatsoever, at a private audience, in the only presence of the Secretary of State. On the following day, this audience took place and was even simpler than I had imagined. After I handed over to the President my letters, without offering or receiving any of the usual complimentary remarks, he seemed to put aside somewhat his official reserve; he asked me to sit by him and as during my first interview he discussed several subjects entirely foreign to business, neglecting however no opportunity to make me feel how pleased he was to see me as Minister of the King of France to the United States. This most friendly welcome on the part of the President is a favorable omen for the future and I find in this simple procedure which he has chosen for the reception of public Ministers a few advantages, particularly with regard to a future mission from England which I shall have the honor of discussing in my next dispatch.

The Secretary of State, Mr. Jefferson, who left the President's house with me, and with whom I talked for almost half an hour, did not mention business either and under the present circumstances I thought it better not to press the point believing that it would be to my advantage to wait and see. However this reserve will not be observed if anything of importance for the service of the King should come up.

TERNANT

(Editor's translation. Turner, p. 43, 44, 45.)

TERNANT TO MONTMORIN

Philadelphia, October 24, 1791

SIR:

I left for Virginia on the 10th of this month, as I had the honor of informing you in my despatch of the 9th, and during the three days I spent at the President's house I was the object of every conceivable attention. The President has always been very appreciative of personal attention; he seemed to be much pleased that I had come especially to visit him in his country estate which he calls his farm. I had hoped that he would give me the opportunity of discussing business with him; but on this point I found him almost as reticent at home as when he appears in an official capacity. While taking a walk, the day before my departure, he indicated that he had a keen desire to see some action taken with regard to the decree of June 2. Thereupon I presented about the same observations as I had to the Secretary of the Treasury; these remarks were communicated to you in my despatch of the 9th. The President seemed to appreciate them, but at once he drew back into himself and changed the subject, so that, contrary to my intention, I was unable to make him talk on the project of negotiations with which the expected Minister from England may be entrusted. Mr. Jefferson arrived at Mount Vernon the day before the President's departure and, in the evening, I had a rather long talk with him but I was not able to bring up the matter of business. This reserve under circumstances which lent themselves so naturally to complete confidence, strengthened my conviction that the Secretary of State is of the opinion that the decree of June 2 puts the King in the necessity of making proposals to the United States, and that these proposals will give the edge to the Federal government in negotiating a new treaty, particularly if England, as is expected, presents similar proposals. . . .

TERNANT

(*Editor's translation*. Turner, p. 60, 61.)

Chateaubriand

Chateaubriand arrived in America, at the beginning of July 1791, with the great project of discovering the Northwestern passage. He probably saw Washington about July 15, and there is no real reason to doubt the authenticity of his account. The rest of his itinerary offers more problems which have been often discussed. On this point, see G. Chinard *L'Exotisme américain dans l'œuvre de Chateaubriand,* Paris, 1918. He gave a first version of his visit to Washington in his *Voyage en Amérique,* published in 1826. The text translated here was taken from the *Mémoires d'Outre-Tombe.* It is substantially the same, but is evidently a revision and for this reason was preferred.

A YOUNG ROYALIST VISITS A
REPUBLICAN PRESIDENT

When I arrived in Philadelphia General Washington was away and I had to wait for him about a week. I saw him riding in a state coach drawn by four spirited horses. Washington according to the ideas I had entertained was of necessity a new Cincinnatus; Cincinnatus in a four in hand, this sight was somewhat disturbing to my conception of a republic of the year of Rome 296. Could Washington the dictator be anything but a rustic driving his oxen with a goad and holding the stilt of his plough? However, when I presented to him my letter of introduction I recognized the simplicity of the old Roman.

A small house, just like the adjacent houses, was the palace of the President of the United States; no guard, not even a footman. I knocked; a young maid servant opened the door. I asked her whether the general was at home; she answered that he was. I added that I had a letter for him. The girl asked for my name; it is not an easy one to pronounce in English and she could not repeat it. She then said gently: "Walk in, Sir. *Entrez, Monsieur,*" and she walked ahead of me through one of these narrow passageways which form the vestibule of English houses. Finally she showed me into a parlor and bade me wait for the general.

I was not perturbed; I feel no awe when confronted by great wealth or a great human soul.

A few minutes later, the General came in: a tall man, he appeared calm and cold rather than noble. The engravings give a good likeness of him. Silently I handed him my letter; he opened it, glanced at the signature which he read aloud, exclaiming: "Colonel Armand!" Such was the name which the Marquis de la Rouërie had signed and by which the General used to call him.

We sat down. I explained, the best I could, the purpose of my journey. He answered in English or French monosyllables and listened to me as if somewhat astonished. I noticed it and said rather petulantly: "But it is less difficult to discover the north-west passage than to create a nation as you have done." Thereupon he exclaimed: "Well, well, young man! *Bien, bien, jeune homme!*" giving me his hand. Then he invited me to dine with him the following day and we parted company.

94

I did not fail to keep the appointment. We were only five or six guests, and our conversation turned on the French Revolution. The General showed us a key from the Bastille. These keys, as I have already mentioned, were rather silly toys which were sent around at that time. Three years later, the same distributors of hardware could have sent to the President the bolt of the prison in which was confined the king who gave liberty both to France and America. If Washington had seen the conquerors of the Bastille lying in the Paris gutters, he would have had much less reverence for that relic. What was important and strong in the Revolution was not the outcome of these murderous orgies. At the time of the Revocation of the Edict of Nantes, the same mob from the Faubourg-Saint-Antoine demolished the protestant temple at Charenton just as enthusiastically as later they sacked the Church at Saint-Denis in 1793.

I took leave of my host at ten o'clock in the evening and never saw him again. He departed the next day and I resumed my journey.

Such was my meeting with the soldier citizen, the liberator of a world. Washington had gone down to his rest before my steps ever attracted any attention. I passed on before his eyes, unknown among other men. He was in all his glory; I was buried in complete obscurity. Perchance my name lingered in his memory for not even one day. Yet, happy am I that he cast his eyes upon my face, for my whole life has been quickened by this single glance. There is a sort of virtue in the eyes of a great man.

WASHINGTON AND BONAPARTE

Only yesterday did Bonaparte die. Since I have just knocked upon Washington's door, drawing a parallel between the founder of the United States and the Emperor of the French comes naturally to my mind, and so much easier will it be for me to pen these lines as Washington himself has passed away. When Ercilla was singing and fighting in

95

Chili, he interrupted the course of his relation in order to narrate the death of Dido; so will I stop at the beginning of my travel through Pennsylvania in order to compare Washington and Bonaparte. I could have saved this parallel for the time when I met Napoleon; but were I to meet with death before reaching the year 1814 in this chronicle, posterity would never hear what I have to say about these two agents of divine Providence. I remember Castelnau: when he was an ambassador in England, as I am, he wrote, as I do now, in London, part of the memoirs of his life. On the last page of book VII, he wrote for his son: "I shall elaborate on this fact in book VIII," and the eighth book of the Memoirs of Castelnau was never written. This is a warning to make use of life while it lasts.

Washington, unlike Bonaparte, does not belong to a race of supermen, and his personality does not strike one with wonder. He did not act upon a huge stage and never came to grips with the ablest captains and the mightiest monarchs of his time. He did not rush from Memphis to Vienna, from Cadiz to Moscow; with a handful of citizens he fought, in the narrow circle of their domestic hearths, upon a land still unfamed. He waged none of the battles that renewed the triumphs of Arbela or Pharsalia; he did not overthrow any thrones to build new ones out of their ruins; he sent no warning to the kings at his door,

Qu'ils se font trop attendre et qu'Attila s'ennuie.

The deeds of Washington were wrapped in silence; he was slow to act; it might be said that he felt himself entrusted with the liberty of the future and was afraid of placing it in jeopardy. This hero of unprecedented kind did not carry the burden of his own destiny, but the destiny of his own country; he could not risk that which did not belong to him; but from that deep humility what a light was to burst forth! Search the forests through which flashed the sword of Washington: what will be found? Tombs? No; a world. For

96

a monument on the field of battle, Washington erected the United States.

Bonaparte has none of the traits of this stern American: he fought among the din of battles upon an age-old land; he wished to create nothing but his own fame; he was the instrument of his own fate only. He seemed to know that his mission would be of short duration, that the torrent which streamed forth from such a height would soon run dry and he hastened to enjoy and exhaust his glory as one does swift passing youth. Like the Homeric gods, he strove within four steps to reach the end of the world. He appeared on all the shores; he made haste to write his name in the annals of every nation; he bestowed crowns upon his family and his soldiers; he rushed into building his monuments, his laws and his soldiers. Leaning over the world, he overthrew the kings with one hand and with the other knocked down the revolutionary giant; but while he crushed anarchy, he also smothered liberty and at the end lost his own on his last battlefield.

Both received the deserts of their work. Washington raised a nation to independence; a serene magistrate, he breathed his last breath in his own house, amidst the regrets of his fellow citizens and the veneration of the nations of the world.

Bonaparte robbed a country of her independence; a fallen emperor, he was hurled into exile and the frightened world could not believe that even with the Ocean as a jailor his prison was strong enough to hold him. He died: this news proclaimed at the door of the palace from which the conqueror had given the signal for so many funerals, did not make the passers-by pause or wonder: what loss could the citizens deplore?

The republic of Washington survives; the empire of Bonaparte has been destroyed. Washington and Bonaparte are the products of democracy: both were the sons of liberty; the first remained faithful to her; the second betrayed her.

Washington represented the needs, the ideas, the lights and the opinions of his time; he helped and never hindered the growth of man's understanding; he willed what it was his duty to will, the very thing for which he had received the call. Hence the coherence and the perpetuity of his work. Such a man appeals little to the imagination because he was so well balanced and fused his life with the life of his country. His glory is the heritage of civilization; his fame rises as one of these public shrines from which flows a spring bountiful and inexhaustible.

Bonaparte also could have enriched a common domain; he was leading the most intelligent, the bravest and the most brilliant among the nations of the earth. What rank would he not occupy now, had he combined magnanimity with his heroic qualities and, being Washington and Bonaparte at the same time, he had made liberty the residuary legatee of his glory?

But this giant did not relate his own destiny to the destinies of his contemporaries: through his genius he belonged to modern times; by his ambition he was linked with an obsolete age and he failed to realize that the miracles of his life transcended the value of a crown and that such a gothic ornament would not fit him. At times he anticipated the future, at otherc times he retired into the past; but whether going up or down the stream of time, through his prodigious strength he drew along with him or pushed back its waters. In his eyes men were only a means to achieve power; there was no common ground between their happiness and his own; he had promised to make them free and he put them in chains; he stood alone among them and they drew away from him. The kings of Egypt placed their funereal pyramids, not among fertile fields but amidst sterile sands. Their gigantic tombs rise from the desert as an image of eternity: such is the monument built by Bonaparte to his fame. (*Editor's translation.*)

Moreau de Saint-Méry

The diary of Moreau de Saint-Méry was discovered and published by Professor Stewart L. Mims, *Voyage aux Etats-Unis de l'Amérique, 1793-1798.* Yale University Press, 1913.

It is a most valuable chronicle of the life led by the French émigrés in Philadelphia, but contains very few extensive comments. The former colonial administrator and public official of the city of Paris had opened a book shop where émigrés of different persuasion used to meet to exchange gossip and occasionally to quarrel. Short as they are, the comments here reproduced leave no doubt on Moreau's admiration for the republican virtues of the President. A readable, but still inadequate biography of Moreau de Saint-Méry has appeared recently: A. Elicona, *Un colonial sous la Révolution*. Paris, 1934.

WASHINGTON OPENS THE SESSION OF CONGRESS

Nov. 1794.

I went to see Washington entering the Hall of Congress and to listen to his opening address. What a simplicity, and how natural everything was! But it was Washington! But it was a gathering of the representatives of a nation that had conquered its liberty! What vast and grandiose ideas in surroundings so unpretentious! How these republican ways appealed to the mind and elevated the heart! What destinies did they not foretell for this part of the world! (*Editor's translation.* Mims, p. 192.)

AN OPENING SESSION OF CONGRESS

I wish to say a word about the ceremonial observed for the opening of Congress.

The two Houses having the quorum required by the Constitution send word to the President who fixes the day when he will meet them.

Then the two Chambers gather in the House of Representatives; the President of the Senate sits on the right and the Speaker of the House of Representatives on the left.

The Senate enters in a body and then the House of Representatives becomes the Congress. The members of the Senate sit in armchairs in the lower part of the hemicycle.

When the Senators arrive, the Representatives stand; they are led from the door of the hall to the inner part by a sergeant at arms carrying the mace.

At twelve o'clock, ordinarily (such was the case on November 19, 1794) Washington arrived in his four-in-hand in which he rode alone. His three servants and his coachman wore a white livery with red facings and collars.

Seven constables with white rods marched ahead of the carriage and were preceded by 14 other constables.

When the President enters the room everybody stands. He sits in the armchair ordinarily occupied by the Speaker of the House, then he rises after a short time and takes place between the two presidents of the Senate and the House, but on the highest step. After bowing, he delivers his address during which he stands as well as the whole Congress.

The Ambassadors have chairs on the right of Washington, but on the floor of the hall. They remain seated during the address.

When the address is over, Washington gives a copy of it to each of the two presidents, then he walks out and goes back to his house with the same escort as when he arrived.

Washington was clad in black, his back hair was held in a silk bag, he carried a chapeau-bras and wore a sword. There is no applause when the President arrives or leaves.

The silence which prevails in the galleries of Congress is worthy of the highest praise. (*Editor's translation*. Mims, p. 376-377.)

Ph. Guilbert & Antoine Michel Servan

The following extract is taken from the *Correspondance entre quelques hommes honnêtes, ou Lettres philosophiques, Politiques et Critiques sur les événemens et les ouvrages du tems. . Publiées par une Société de gens de lettres.* 2 vols, Lausanne, 1794. The authors were men of good will rather than of talent. Their views were moderate and liberal. Their portrait of Washington sums up the views of the contemporaries, but more than any author of the time they insist on the main characteristic of Washington, the extraordinary *unity* of the man. At the same time, they probably reflected the views expressed around them on the great American hero and particularly on his Plutarchian virtues.

A PLUTARCHIAN PARALLEL

At least, Sir, it seems to me that your Englishman does justice to *Vashington*. To anticipate that the United States will disintegrate after his death is to admit that he truly binds them together, and when a private citizen is entrusted in succession by his fellow citizens with military power and political authority, he receives a tribute that raises him to the same height as the great citizens of ancient times. Your author is right, and since he writes in order to clarify our estimate of things and men, it may not be amiss to discuss a while this American.

Shall I dare say it, Sir, it seems to me that Europe has paid too little attention to the merits of *Vashington*. Though it may be difficult to recognize in *Vashington* any of the qualities which people call heroic or sublime, the combination of those he possesses and the way he employed them make him stand among all the men famous or renowned in our age as the most *complete,* in my opinion, that has appeared in the four parts of the world. He is not the greatest general, nor the most resourceful statesman, but he is a *whole* man, and in the words of Montagne, he is not one of these great men who are great only in spots and places." One does not realize fully enough, Sir, the value of such a rare *unity*, for in everything men pay much more attention to what stands out and becomes *prominent* than to what is closely bound together so as to form a *whole*. This precious *unity* results from a perfect equilibrium between mind and character, between ideas and passions, between what one wills and what one can do; this *unity* of all the things which constitute a man, is what makes

101

a true sage, a man worthy of being called great, if ever such a name can be applied to human frailty.

While indulging in speculations upon this subject, I have entertained myself now and then in trying to discover between *Aratus,* the famous and ancient chief of the *Achaean League* and *Vashington,* the modern chief of the *American League,* resemblances rather remarkable notwithstanding the many differences introduced by time and place in human affairs. I even thought in comparing these two great subjects, that the resemblances were to be found in the men while the differences came from the things: that *Vashington* resembles more *Aratus* than the *Achaean League* resembles the United States.

These sorts of comparisons between times and men seem to bring nature down to this *unity* mentioned above, a unity always gratifying to the human mind because it helps in measuring diversity itself. Therefore with your permission, I shall try to bring *Aratus* and *Vashington* under the same standard.

Both of them, at the beginning of their career started from a condition most remote from their ultimate dignity: *Vashington* was born in non-official and almost obscure surroundings; *Aratus* was born in a worse station, an exile from his ancestral land.

Both of them entertained the same design, to bring back liberty not only to their own country, but to all the neighboring countries, and to unite them in a single body by forming a confederation. Both carried out their plans almost through the same virtues, the same talents, the same labors; both won most completely the confidence of their fellow-citizens, a result already very difficult to achieve by modest people in a republic as well as in a monarchy, but a miraculous accomplishment when this confidence is obtained from several republics, all of them envious of the man whom only one of them can claim. I do not know of any man who could share this honor with Washington, except perhaps the Prince of Orange in the United Provinces.

Aratus and *Vashington,* in their various fortunes, displayed the same kind of courage, not the impetuous courage that attacks repeatedly and overcomes every obstacle unless one is killed in the attempt, but courage accompanied with patience, steadfastness, which neither the resistance of the enemies nor the praise nor even the criticism of friends sets aflame, the kind of courage that knows how to wait and to prepare for future successes in the midst of present reverses. *Aratus* and *Vashington,* both raised equally to the full of civil and military powers, both of them in position to make ill use of them, and both suspected of entertaining such an ambition, resigned these powers with the same sublime modesty and simplicity. They accepted them back only to resign them again. Both of them, finally, either because of the magnanimity of their character, or because of their political wisdom, became, in a way, the masters of their fellow-citizens, simply by striving persistently to remain their equals.

Through a rather curious conformity *Aratus* was able to preserve the Achaean League only by contracting an alliance with King Ptolemeus, in order to assist the efforts of King Antigonus, almost as Washington sought and found the preservation of the United States in an alliance with the King of France against the King of England: lastly, even the famous expedition of Philadelphia had a precedent in the life of *Aratus*: just as *Vashington* was to do, he retreated before the enemy, allowed them to pass over *Mount Gerania,* let them enter Peloponesus and capture the important city of *Pellena* in which the enemy army was caught as in a net. People said at the time that the English army had not captured *Philadelphia,* but that *Philadelphia* had captured the English army: the same saying could have been used about the expedition of *Pellena.*

I shall not draw this parallel further, because one must be very cautious when comparing things which are close to us; a greater circumspection must be observed when dealing with objects which are so remote. However, I have said enough and mentioned a sufficient number of resemblances to establish the fame of *Vashington* and to increase *Aratus'* fame. These last words may seem very bold; but please remark, Sir, that when Plutarch lauded *Aratus* he was considering him through an interval of time of three or four hundred years, while *Vashington* is praised by his contemporaries during his lifetime: this makes an enormous difference. If it were permitted to apply geometrical formulas to moral quantities, one might say that the praise given to famous men varies in a compound ratio to their qualities and the space of time which separate them from us. The greater the interval, the more these qualities increase; the smaller it is, the smaller they grow. According to this formula how superior to the head of the ancient league would the modern one appear. But let us change the subject; it is not possible to express human worth with figures, unless perhaps when dealing with people who rank a mere cypher. (*Editor's translation.* Correspondance, vol. II, p. 59-64.)

Genet

Citizen Genet needs no introduction. His mission to America constitutes the most lamentable episode in the history of the relations between France and the United States. His dispatches are filled with vituperations against the President and unbelievable expressions of self-satisfaction. However, the full story has never been told, and it is to be hoped that someone will utilize more fully than has been done heretofore the Genet papers now deposited in the Library of Congress. It may not be amiss to recall that Genet's attitude and conduct were severely criticized and formally blamed by his own government. On his life, see M. Minnegerode, *Jefferson, Friend of France, 1793. The career of Edmond-Charles Genet.* New York, 1929.

"OLD WASHINGTON" AND A FIERY PLENIPOTENTIARY
GENET TO MINISTER OF FOREIGN AFFAIRS

Philadelphia, June 19, 1793.

. . . . Everything has succeeded beyond my hopes: the true Republicans triumph, but old Washington, *le vieux Washington,* a man very different from the character emblazoned in history, cannot forgive me for my successes and the eagerness with which the whole city rushed to my house, while a mere handful of English merchants went to congratulate him on his proclamation. He puts thousand of obstacles in my way, and makes it necessary for me to urge secretly a convocation of Congress a majority of which, led by the best brains of the American Union, will be decidedly on our side. (*Editor's translation.* Turner, p. 217)

Philadelphia, September 19, 1793.

. . . We have lost a precious time, but it is still possible to make up for it. This circumstance, Citizen Minister, is very fortunate, and contributes much in upholding the courage of our friends: their zeal is strong, they will support us with enthusiasm and will protect our rights in the next Congress, in spite of General Washington who sacrifices these rights to our enemies and who will never forgive me for finding in his people enough support to put our treaties into effect against his wishes. This friend of Lafayette, who ostentatiously decorates his reception room with medallions of Capet and his family, who has received from the so-called Regent letters brought by Noailles and Talon and continues to see these scoundrels, calls me Anarchist, Jacobin and threatens me with recall, because I am not subservient to a Federalist party unwilling to do anything for us and whose only aim is to establish Monocracy in this country (*Editor's translation.* Turner, p. 242-243.)

Genet's successor was no less virulent than the too famous "citizen." This was the period of the "great schism" to borrow the happy term used by Mr. Bernard Faÿ. The following letter, written after the ratification of Jay's treaty, needs no elaboration, except that many of the French agents then in this country, and particularly Fauchet, blamed much more the "government" and the "cabinet" than Washington himself. The most serious and constant reproach addressed to him being that he was a tool in the hands of unscrupulous politicians.

THE SHADOW OF A GREAT MAN

ADET TO THE COMMITTEE OF PUBLIC SAFETY

Philadelphia, Fructidor 16 (September 2, 1795).
The Third Year of the French Republic
One and Indivisible.

The Minister Plenipotentiary of the French Republic to the United States, to the Representatives of the People, Members of the Committee of Public Safety.

CITIZEN REPRESENTATIVES: My conjectures have been verified; the President has just countersigned the dishonor of his old age and the shame of the United States: he has ratified the Treaty of Commerce and Amity with Great Britain, and Hammond, the English Minister, has left New York for Europe on Fructidor 1rst, with the definite pledge of the blind submission of Washington to the supreme will of George.

Neither the objections of Mr. Randolph and his friends, nor the resolutions of several Town Meetings, nor the interests of his allies have been able to shake him from his first resolve; the feelings of subservience which bound him to England, repressed for twenty years by his ambition only, are now displayed in all their strength. Gratified to rule as a master over people who respect him as a father, and believe their own destinies bound up with his, Washington wishes to make amend for his wrongs to George III and, at his death bed, delivers back, as a herd of cattle, men whom he had so to speak taken on lease.

What else could be expected from a man who did not hear without tremor the proclamation of the independence of his country and who, ten days before, had written to his wife: "I love my King, as you know; what soldier, what honest man would not love him? How cruel it is to be considered a traitor to such a good king. If he could read in the bottom of my heart, he would do me justice; I feel certain that posterity will do it."

To make use of every circumstance in order to reach supreme power, such was his only aim; his love for his country and the sublimity of the cause he had to defend were powerless to stir a heart that could be moved only by the glamor of ambition. Please read, Citizen Representatives, the enclosed extract and you will be convinced of the truth of this assertion.

I should like to send you in their entirety those letters of Washington of which you will find here only a few fragments; but they are too voluminous to be copied; soon they will be printed and then I shall forward them to you. What these letters will demonstrate I have already heard from several contemporaries of Washington, from the respectable Samuel Adams, Governor of Massachusetts, from Mr. Beykley, secretary of Congress and from many others. They have observed the man at close range and know what he really is.

Stubborn in his resolutions, athirst for power, eager to keep it, rabidly fond of false praise, responsive to flattery, he has rejected the counsels of men truly interested in his glory and in the good of their country. He became tired of the glorious rest which he enjoyed after the war, and he scorned to continue as the equal of the men his sword had liberated. It was not enough for him to be first in the esteem of his fellow citizens, to honor his time by offering a new example of the virtues of Cincinnatus; much inferior to the reputation that credulous writers, flatterers and the schemers who surrounded him have complacently built up for him, ignoring the true glory which urges great men forward, he stupidly traded it for the false glamor of power. Through Hamilton, he brought into being this Constitution which today governs the United States of America; on them he has superimposed the personal authority of a President, certain that under this title he would gather in his hands in a single bunch all the reins of a government to which he could not pay obedience and more particularly which he did not want to share with anybody.

Ah! if as ambitious as Cæsar he had been endowed with the same heart and talents and had known the same successes, his times and posterity mercifully covering his mistakes with a veil of pity would have set off his virtues in their full splendor. But what has he done to obliterate the memory of those errors? Nothing. He is one of the offsprings of popular enthusiasm, blind to good and evil, vice and virtue, who manage to survive as long as the darkness of error prevails and are bound to disappear in the full light of truth.

The day has come for the United States when, at least for the thinking few, shorn of all the prestige which surrounded him, Washington, this colossal hero, this lasting pride of America is but a wretch whose strength has been exaggerated by a superstitious credulity as if by a magic power. He is no longer the savior of his country, but an ambitious man who betrayed a people unreservedly delivered into his hand by excessive loyalty. Truths held back by a consensus of opinion, because people hesitated to hurt a man who deserved some gratitude and in whom one could suppose some good intentions, are now rushing forth like a torrent. It is known that Washington became a soldier by accident, but that he was not a statesman; that he never was able to grasp large designs; that his narrow imagination could never conceive any idea requiring the slightest intellectual effort; that it always was a necessity for him, during the war, during his presidency and even when dealing with his own private affairs, to borrow outside assistance and that he only knew how to copy slavishly what a helping hand had drafted for him. One knows that Colonel Humphrey in the army, Colonel Hamilton during his presidency, his nephew d'Andriger (Dandridge) in his private affairs have always lent him the resources of their intelligence. It is known, finally, that if George has a Pitt, Washington has a Hamilton and that the passions of his Minister, combined with his own, his affections and leanings, will drive America back under the yoke of England, thus bringing about a state of things fatal to this country, to France and perhaps to Europe, unless it is modified by some new political combination. It is your business, Citizen Representatives to know men and events; in consequence, I deemed it my duty to outline for you the main traits of Washington's character from the data I obtained and the informations given by several reliable people. You may feel somewhat astonished that the people of America, to whom is attributed a larger measure of enlightenment and knowledge than they really possess, could be deceived for such a long time by the mere shadow of a great man; but let me remind you that if Robespierre had not been a cruel and sanguinary tyrant, his sway over public opinion would not have been so easily destroyed, and yet what did he amount to in the Committee of Public Safety?

Salut et Fraternité

PIERRE ADET.

(*Editor's translation.* Turner, p. 776-779.)

La Rochefoucauld-Liancourt

The relation of the duke of La Rochefoucauld-Liancourt has been severely judged by Mr. Bernard Faÿ: "huit volumes in octavo, bien lourds, bien monotones, bien pédants." They appeared in France as *Voyage dans les Etats-Unis d'Amérique, fait en 1795, 1796, et 1797*. Paris, an VII. Two editions were printed in London almost at the same time: *Travels through the United States of North America.* London 1799, 2 vols in 4° and 4 vols in 8°. An edition of La Rochefoucauld-Liancourt's diary by M. Jean Marchand was in print last August and it is to be hoped that it will appear shortly. It is naturally much less pedantic than the relation itself. In spite of his obvious faults, La Rochefoucauld-Liancourt seems to have been a somewhat grouchy but objective observer and his book contains much information of real value on the state of public opinion in America during these critical years. He did not meet Washington, nor did he visit Mount Vernon.

A CRITICISM OF HOUDON'S STATUE OF WASHINGTON

The Capitol is erected on a point of this hill which commands the town. This edifice, which is extremely vast, is constructed on the plan of the "Maison Quarrée" at Nismes, but on a much more extensive scale. The attics of the Maison Quarrée have undergone an alteration in the Capitol, to suit them for the convenience of the public offices of every denomination, which, thus perfectly secure against all accidents from fire, lie within reach of the tribunals, the executive council, the governor, the general assembly, who all sit in the Capitol, and draw to it a great afflux of people. This building, which is entirely of brick, is not yet coated with plaster: the columns, the pilasters, are destitute of bases and capitals: but the interior and exterior cornices are finished, and are well executed. The rest will be completed with more or less speed: but, even in its present unfinished state, this building is, beyond comparison, the finest, the most noble, and the greatest, in all America. The internal distribution of its parts is extremely well adapted to the purposes for which it is destined. It was Mr. Jefferson who, during his embassy in France, sent the model of it. Already it is said to have cost a hundred and seventy thousand dollars; and fifteen thousand more are the estimated sum requisite for completing it and remedying some defects which have been observed in the construction. (*Travels,* IV, p. 299-300.)

In the great central vestibule, which is lighted by a kind of dome contained in the thickness of the roof, has lately been placed a statue of George Washington, voted, ten years since, by the general assembly of Virginia. In addition to the sentiments of gratitude which they felt in common with the rest of America, that body entertained moreover a particular affection for him, together with the pride of having him for their countryman. Since that period the president has acquired new claims to the general approbation and esteem. If he be chargeable with some errors in administration, as I think he is, nevertheless his devotion to the public weal and the purity of his intentions cannot even be suspected: yet it is doubtful whether at the present moment the assembly of Virginia would be inclined to vote him such an honour: at least it is certain that the same unanimity would not prevail on the occasion. This statue was executed by Houdon, one of the first sculptors in France. He undertook a voyage to America five or six years since for the express purpose of making a bust of the president from the life. Although the statue be beautiful, and display even a nobleness in the composition and a likeness in the features, it does not bear the marks of Houdon's talent: one cannot trace in it the hand of him who produced the celestial Diana which constitutes the chief part of that artist's reputation.

Near this statue of the president stands a marble bust of monsieur de la Fayette, voted at the same time by the assembly of Virginia, and also carved by Houdon, but with greater display of ability.

WASHINGTON RETIRES FROM PUBLIC LIFE

On the day preceding my arrival at Boston, the president's proclamation was received there, in which he announces his firm determination of retiring from public life. It is in the month of March next that the four years of his second presidency will expire; and in December of the present year the elections will be held for the choice of a person to be placed at the head of the federal government. It was therefore time that he should announce his resolution, which I cannot otherwise consider than as a serious misfortune for the United States: for the office of president is not so well provided with the means of execution as not to require some accession of strength from the popularity of the man who holds it, and from the confidence reposed in him by his fellow-citizens. Now, in all the United States, no individual possesses so many claims to the general confidence as George Washington, nor does any individual enjoy it in so high a degree.

That proclamation of the president, besides what relates to his resignation, contains also political counsels to the citizens of the United States.—No man entertains a higher respect than I do for the president's merit and virtues; none is more firmly convinced that the sole object of his conduct has invariably been the good of his country; but when a man is a native of France, he must have that opinion established on very strong grounds indeed, if he do not, in one part of the proclamation, discover a marked antipathy to France, and a predilection for England, which bear a much stronger resemblance to party-spirit than to the spirit of justice, or even, I will venture to say, to sound policy. I do not mean that any blame can attach to him for the advice which he gives to his countrymen not to become dependent on any other nation: but it appears that this counsel, delivered simply and in general terms, would preserve all its force, its propriety, its justice; whereas, offered as it is in such ample extent, and with the characters which accompany its development, one cannot be surprized that the president's enemies find in it a subject for censure: and among those who esteem and respect his virtues without feeling the influence of party-spirit, there are few, I believe, who would not have wished that this over-long article had been treated in a different manner. Even the other parts of the proclamation, which are not liable to the reproach of impropriety or party spirit, are justly taxable

112

with diffuseness and unnecessary length. All the principles indeed are true, and the counsels good: but they would have been equally so, and would have appeared more so, if they had been delivered with conciseness and simplicity. I have further heard it observed that the advices contained in that proclamation are unseasonably given. It is (say those who censure it) in vacating the chair after the expiration of his term, that his adieux would have come at their proper time: but they are premature when the man who thus takes his leave of the public has yet six months to exercise his functions.

That proclamation, as may reasonably be expected, meets with admirers who extol the very parts which most deserve censure, as well as censurers who condemn in it what is entitled to nought but praise.

This resignation of the president, which was doubted through all America a fortnight ago, seems however to produce no sensation at Boston; it engrosses no greater share of the general attention than any other article of intelligence; and after the first day it ceased to be a topic of conversation. The defects and the merits of the proclamation are equally buried in silence. Does this indifference with which so important an event is viewed at Boston arise from the circumstance of the people's minds being wholly engrossed by interested pursuits, so as to leave no room for any other object? or is it the offspring of constitutional apathy? These are questions which I shall be better able to determine when I have seen a greater number of people and visited different places. In the mean time I am not the less surprized at what I here observe. (*Travels*, V, p. 206-209.)

Plane

Lavater had many disciples in France. At the beginning of the nineteenth century, physiognomy became a fad as well as a subject for more serious studies. The physiognomical analysis of Washington's features is here given as a curiosity and as an indication of his fame: so great a man could not be omitted from the list of "characters" who, in various capacities, and in various degrees had influenced the development of mankind. It appeared in *Physiologie, ou l'Art de Connaître les Hommes, sur leur Physionomie. Ouvrage extrait de Lavater . . . avec des observations sur les traits de quelques personnages qui ont figuré dans la révolution française.* Par J.M.Plane. A. Meudon, de l'Imprimerie de P.S.C.Demailly. L'an 1797 (v.s.). The other "physionomies" appearing on the plate are easily identified from the text as Bonaparte, Sully and Franklin. However I cannot identify with certainty N°. 1, and the description provides little definite information, except that the man portrayed there could "master his passions".

A PHYSIOGNOMICAL ANALYSIS OF WASHINGTON

One will notice in the features of N° 4, the oblong shape which, when not too angular, is always a sign of firmness and judgment. In this physiognomy, one will recognize the marks of an extraordinary genius, capable of forming the plan of a revolution never to be forgotten, and of an heroic genius capable of seeing it through. The courage which appears on this face seems to be tempered with wisdom and unassuming modesty. It is full of noble audacity, an audacity which never yields to the heat of passions, but always remains self-possessed because it is conscious of its strength. (*Editor's translation.* Plane, p. 331).

Crèvecœur

In the first French edition of his *Lettres d'un Cultivateur Américain,* Paris, 1784, Crèvecœur had hardly mentioned Washington. In the edition published in 1787 in three volumes, the last one of which never appeared in English, the whole of Letter XI treats of Washington from page 250 to 314. It is much too long to be reproduced here and to a large extent consists of a translation of letters and proclamations of Wash-

ington. More personal are the views expressed by Crèvecœur in his *Voyage dans la Haute Pensylvanie et dans l'état de New York, par un membre adoptif de la Nation Onéida.* Paris, an IX, 1801. The dedication, obviously written before Crèvecœur heard of the death of the first President, was kept by him as a last tribute to the great man he was so proud of having known personally. As a frontispiece to the first volume Crèvecœur reproduced the medallion of Washington made by Madame de Bréhan in 1789. On Crèvecœur and for an excellent bibliography of his publications, see Howard C. Rice, Le *Cultivateur Américain. Etude sur l'œuvre de Saint-John de Crèvecœur.* Paris, 1933.

WASHINGTON IS NOMINATED FOR IMMORTALITY

To His Excellency

GEORGE WASHINGTON

The man who, in 1774, saw you appear as the representative of the State of Virginia at the First Congress, known under the name of Venerable, which was so wise and steadfast in its conduct of the revolution.

The man who, in 1775, heard you called to the command of the armies by the vote of this same Congress and of your Country, so that you might save their liberty and their independence.

The man, who, as many others did, deemed your conduct generous as well as sublime at the critical time of the disbanding of the continental army.

The man who could not but peruse with admiration the letter you addressed to the Governors of the thirteen States, a letter worthy of being handed down to posterity.

The man whose heart shared the emotion of the citizens of New York when, after taking possession of the city and restoring its government, you left it and went to Annapolis.

The man who heard the people through the countryside and the cities pour forth their thankful blessings upon you along your eighty league long journey.

The man who witnessed the memorable day when, having raised your country to the rank of a nation, you resigned your military commission into the hands of the Chief of the Union, to become once more a private citizen.

The man who saw you, during your years of retirement, no less great, no less worthy of being an example, when you were developing the navigation of the Potomac and Shenandoah rivers, and administered your vast agricultural estate, than when you were at the head of the armies;

The man who happened to be in Philadelphia at the time you were elected President of the Federal Convention, an enlightened body to whom the United States are beholden for their wise government;

The man who, in 1789, saw you, a new Cincinnatus, regretfully relinquish your rural pursuits to become the Supreme Chief of the Union, in compliance with the wishes of your fellow citizens, a public office you resigned after eight years of the most wise and magnanimous administration;

The man who, in 1797, saw you for the second time, a private citizen once more, devote your leisure to the care of the fields;

And at last, the man whom you so long honored with your esteem and kindness, deeply moved by the sublime virtues you practiced during your whole life, this man begs you to accept that this unworthy book be inscribed to you, as the only public testimony he can proffer of his deep veneration.

S.D.C.

CRÈVECŒUR'S LAST TRIBUTE TO WASHINGTON

You may have heard praise of the cider of this district, a huge quantity of which is sold yearly in the Southern States. In Georgia I drank some which seemed to me to taste even better than here. Two months ago, when the orchards were in full bloom, General Washington came to New Ark and I had the pleasure of offering him some: he found it almost as delicately flavored as the cider they make in Virginia from wild apples and which is known as Crabb-Apple-Cyder.

What! Mr. Herman exclaimed, you had the privilege of entertaining this great man in your own house and of conversing with him. The deep interest, the respect his name and virtues have always evoked have impelled me, since I arrived on this continent, to find some way of being introduced to him. But my effort have been of no avail; I only caught a glimpse of him in church. Luckier than I, a young business man from St. Malo whose voyage across the Ocean had no other object, although entrusted with an interesting mission by an agricultural society, had the privilege of being introduced to him, and he was even invited to dinner in his house. All of which took him about ten or twelve days and then he sailed back directly for his native land. A painter he had brought along with him, selected in church a seat opposite the General and painted of him a very good likeness. If you know of some particulars about his private life, I would be ever so grateful if you could let me hear them, for everything concerning the deportment, the habits and ways of life of such a famous man are of tremendous import. As for his public life, I read with deep interest what History has already consigned in its annals.

This is what I heard and what I myself know, Mr. G. answered. No one ever appreciated better than General Washington the value of time and the art of making use of it. He is a hard worker, yet he is no slave to his work. He used to say that by doing regularly what should be done, and not by doing too much at one time, can one accomplish a great deal.—Every day of the year, he rises at five in the morning; as soon as he is up, he dresses, then prays reverently to God. A while later, he visits his horses, carefully looks them over, often has them taken out, then gives orders to the grooms. After his visit to the stables, he retires to his study where he works until breakfast time. At this meal, he most usually has tea and eats corn cakes which he butters himself. He is not the only one among the Virginians to prefer corn to wheat.—Then, he proceeds to his study, calling in his secretaries and painstakingly examines their work.

His proclamations, his speeches to the two houses of Congress, his letters, answers to the many addresses and letters he receives, are all written by him, as it appears clearly to anyone who is familiar with his style which is marked with characteristic measure and color. His first address as President of the United States is a model of wisdom, of profound and sublime thoughts, rather than rhetorical and eloquent.

Almost every day, he invites to dine with him Congressional delegates, senators, public officials, as well as foreigners who have been introduced to him. Everything that is left over from the meal is sent immediately to the jail to be given to the most needy among the prisoners. This was his constant practice when he resided in New York as President of the United States; and it was while he stayed in that city that I had many opportunities to see him and to get acquainted with his family. He never had any children; those who are seen in his house are the grandsons of his wife whom he married when she was a widow. When I knew him, he never went to the theater without taking them along; often I saw him holding them on his lap.

He is generally sedate and serious, and only after having two or three glasses of wine and when roused by the conversation around him, does his face assume an expression of liveliness. It has been said that during the war, no one ever saw him laugh; that even when he is among his most intimate friends he seldom smiles. His tall stature (he is five feet nine and a half inches tall, English measure), his distant or rather dignified countenance give him a very commanding appearance. He looks much less austere at Madame Washington's teas, where mingling with the crowd, he talks more familiarly with those he knows, and sometimes with the ladies. I have often seen him leave the city, on fine summer days, and accompanied by a few friends take a walk in the country.

The clothes he wears are always made of American material, and on his table he uses linen, plates and utensils from American manufactures whose managers always present him with their new models. On Sundays, he never fails, with his family, to attend divine service. His mind is more sound than brilliant, and his conduct seems to be directed by staunch good sense and well considered judgment rather than by knowledge acquired from books. He was trained for the administration of public affairs in the school of experience and through reflection. During the Revolution he became acquainted with or heard of a great many people and had an opportunity to test their ability, so that he was always fortunate in his choices. However, out of regard for those who were recommended by his friends, he used to make a note of them in a special note-book. I saw him do this on several occasions.

Brave without ostentation, human without being weak, generous but not to excess, how many times, during the Revolution did he not assist unfortunate people and reward courage and brave deeds? How many tears did he not dry silently, secretly and mysteriously? It is a secret revealed only by the voice of gratitude. He united in himself qualities and virtues which are an honor to the man, to the citizen and to the statesman: wisdom and moderation, knowledge, humanity, modesty, all virtues which make him worthy of the esteem and veneration of his fellow citizens and of posterity.

Such was Washington as a General in chief from 1775 to 1783; such was the private citizen from 1783 to 1789; and finally such was the President of the United States, from this last date to his resignation from the Presidency in 1796.

From the time he was called to the head of the continental army, he was fortunate in silencing calumny, in blunting the darts of jealousy, in harmonizing the opinions of his fellow-citizens and through the confidence they placed in him, he was able to direct their efforts toward a single aim, the liberation of his country. This unique success became even more remarkable when the new Constitution was proclaimed.

Ah, who today could tell what might have happened if he had not been elected to the Presidency, by a miraculous and unanimous vote, and particularly if, while this Constitution was still in its cradle, the Supreme Magistrate had not magnetically attracted to himself and concentrated so many unorganized wills, slowly lessening the influence of those who dreaded to see the main interests of the country under the control of a strong government.

England would have given much to prevent this development, and perhaps Spain also. How far could many other people have gone whose habits and principles, competency or wealth have been destroyed by the war. Their number was large. How many did I see eagerly weighing all the probabilities of the non-ratification of this form of government?

I never ponder upon this memorable period, the unexpected turn of things which has endowed this continent with self-government, without giving thanks for this miraculous concatenation of events and circumstances which I watched for a long time with the deep interest and the anxiety of a good citizen. It is probable that having withstood the dangers which accompany radical changes, as well as several crises which followed, this same government having solaced so much unhappiness, fulfilled so many hopes, tapped so many new sources of manufactures, business enterprise and prosperity, will consolidate itself and will deserve at last the respect and gratitude of its people, unless blinded by their passions, by the madness and fury of partisan spirit, they destroy their own handiwork and are buried under its ruins. If this should come to pass, one might despair of human nature, and believe, as many do, that it is not worthy of enjoying the blessings of liberty, in short that a popular and wise government is but an idle fancy. (*Editor's translation.* Crèvecœur, vol. I, p. 257-263.)

IV.

A French Apotheosis of Washington

BONAPARTE
TALLEYRAND
FONTANES

Bonaparte and Washington

Whatever may have been the political motives of the First Consul in ordering a grandiose pageant in the Temple of Mars on the occasion of the death of Washington, his sincere admiration for the American hero cannot be questioned. The ceremony took place on February 8, 1800 in the presence of the Minister of War, Alexandre Berthier, who had known Washington personally and liked to recall that for one day he had served under him in 1781. The flags taken during the campaign of Egypt, the presence of the veterans of the wars of Italy contributed to the splendor and solemnity of the occasion. The orator was Fontanes who three years before had proposed Washington to the leaders of the French republic as an example of republican virtues, and everything seems to indicate that, at least at that time, one of Bonaparte's highest ambition was to become the Washington of France. Grateful acknowledgment is made here to Houghton, Mifflin and Company for their kind permission to use the translation of Talleyrand's report printed in *George Washington,* by Henry Cabot Lodge. Boston, 2 vols, 1889.

WASHINGTON PROPOSED AS AN EXAMPLE TO THE LEADERS OF ANOTHER REPUBLIC

August 22, 1797.

Our Revolution was the offspring of the American Revolution and today the New World can teach a lesson to the Old World which once was its conqueror. One of my friends, a philosopher and a soldier who traveled through the thirteen United States and for a long time served under Washington, aroused my keenest interest when speaking occasionally of the founder of American liberty. His talks convinced me that the French republic needed only men like Washington to make it secure. At the head of his armies as well as of the Senate, in his public as well as his private life, he deserved the love and admiration of his fellow citizens. His noble character easily curbed all factions and there are almost as many in America as in France. But if it had come to a choice between the factions by which his country was torn, undoubtedly he would not have favored the levellers, the murderers or the *Jacobins* of America. He knew only too well that at any time and in any country it is more dangerous to have such people for allies than for enemies. His moral and political principles would have prevented him from allying the banner of liberty to those of brigands and assassins. The friend whom I mentioned in the beginning told me the other day what the hero of the New World thought about this subject:

"When the rumor of some royalist conspiracy spread through America, I used to observe Washington closely. He was never hasty in accepting such rumors; he was ever as calm as wisdom itself and as simple as virtue. Fear magnifies everything, he said, and the populace enjoys alarms. But there are some faults which must never contaminate the man entrusted with the fortunes of a great people. After all, the enemies I most distrust are not those whose hearts remain loyal to King George; if their principles must be condemned, their characters can be respected. The most patriotic Englishmen do not persecute the few Scotchmen who remain faithful to the house of the Stuarts. The steadfast convictions of a few individuals can be respected as long as they do not endanger public peace. But I distrust some perverse and wily men who were among the first to march with my colors and who, carried away by passion, keep urging the populace to violence and dare to accuse Washington of not loving liberty warmly enough."

A few days after these declarations made by a great man, the traitor Arnold, who was considered as the most zealous

republican, betrayed America and sold himself to England.
(*Editor's translation. Œuvres de M. de Fontanes.* Paris, 1839.
Vol. II, pp. 144-146)

ORDER OF THE DAY TO THE CONSULAR GUARD
AND ALL THE SOLDIERS OF THE REPUBLIC

Washington is dead. This great man fought against tyranny; he established the liberty of his country. His memory
will always be dear to the French people, as it will be to all
free men of the two worlds, and especially to French soldiers,
who, like him and the American soldiers, are fighting for
equality and liberty.

Thereby the First Consul orders, that, during ten days,
black crape shall be suspended from all the the flags and
guidons throughout the Republic

Paris, Pluviose 18, Year 8. *Moniteur.*

"REPORT OF TALLEYRAND, MINISTER
OF FOREIGN AFFAIRS, ON THE OCCASION OF
THE DEATH OF GEORGE WASHINGTON

"A nation which some day will be a great nation, and which
today is the wisest and happiest on the face of the earth,
weeps at the bier of a man whose courage and genius contributed the most to free it from bondage, and elevate it to
the rank of an independent and sovereign power. The regrets
caused by the death of this great man, the memories aroused
by these regrets, and a proper veneration for all that is held
dear and sacred by mankind, impel us to give expression to
our sentiments by taking part in an event which deprives the
world of one of its brightest ornaments, and removes to the
realm of history one of the noblest lives that ever honored
the human race.

"The name of Washington is inseparably linked with a
memorable epoch. He adorned this epoch by his talents and
the nobility of his character, and with virtues that even envy
dared not assail. History offers few examples of such renown.
Great from the outset of his career, patriotic before his

country had become a nation, brilliant and universal despite the passions and political resentments that would gladly have checked his career, his fame is to-day imperishable,—fortune having consecrated his claim to greatness, while the prosperity of a people destined for grand achievements is the best evidence of a fame ever to increase.

"His own country now honors his memory with funeral ceremonies, having lost a citizen whose public actions and unassuming grandeur in private life were a living example of courage, wisdom, and unselfishness; and France, which from the dawn of the American Revolution hailed with hope a nation, hitherto unknown, that was discarding the vices of Europe, which foresaw all the glory that this nation would bestow on humanity, and the enlightenment of governments that would ensue from the novel character of the social institutions and the new type of heroism of which Washington and America were models for the world at large,—France, I repeat, should depart from established usages and do honor to one whose fame is beyond comparison with that of others.

"The man who, amid the decadence of modern ages, first dared believe that he could inspire degenerate nations with courage to rise to the level of republican virtues, lived for all nations and for all centuries: and this nation, which first saw in the life and success of that illustrious man a foreboding of his destiny, and therein recognized a future to be realized and duties to be performed, has every right to class him as a fellow-citizen. I therefore submit to the First Consul the following decree:—

"Bonaparte, First Consul of the republic, decrees as follows:—

"Article 1. A statue is to be erected to General Washington.

"Article 2. This statue is to be placed in one of the squares of Paris, to be chosen by the minister of the interior, and it shall be his duty to execute the present decree." (Lodge, *George Washington,* p. 1-2, n.)

WASHINGTON'S FUNERAL EULOGY
DELIVERED IN THE TEMPLE OF MARS

(Hôtel des Invalides)

Pluviose 20. year VIII (February 8, 1800).

France, ever great and generous enough to acknowledge without fear or jealousy the glory and virtues of a foreign people, today pays a public homage to the spirit of Washington. Today, she discharges the debt of two worlds. A government, of whatever form or opinion, cannot but grant respect to the founder of freedom. Even the country which only a short time ago accused Washington of being a rebel deems the emancipation of America to be one of those events sanctioned by time and by history. Such is the privilege of great characters. They seem to belong so little to their own times that even during their lives their deeds are stamped with the marks of an august and ancient past. Their work, scarcely done attracts already the veneration granted only to works proven by time. The American Revolution, of which we are contemporaries seems actually to be established forever. Washington started it with force and brought it to completion with moderation. He knew how to control it, constantly aiming at a greater prosperity for his country, and this goal is the only one which may justify such extraordinary actions before the tribunal of posterity.

The eulogy of this American hero should be pronounced by the most eloquent voices. I recall with a feeling of admiration mixed with regret that this temple, decorated with every trophy of valour, was erected in a century filled with geniuses and as abundant in great men of letters as in illustrious captains. In those times, the memory of heroes was entrusted to orators whose genius conferred immortality. Today, military glory shines with even a greater splendor, whereas in all countries the glory of the liberal arts is almost extinct. I fear my voice is too faint to be heard on such a solemn and majestic occasion which takes me unawares. At least this voice is undefiled, and since it never flattered any tyranny whatsoever, it has not become unworthy of extolling, for a brief moment, heroism and virtue.

Yea, this funereal and martial ceremony conveys in advance to the bottom of every heart, and better than any word could do, strong and deep emotions. The mourning which the First Consul has ordered for Washington, proclaims to France that the examples he set have not been overlooked. It is less to do honor to the illustrious general than to the benefactor and friend of a great people that funereal crapes are wrapped over our flags and the uniforms of our soldiers. At last they are no longer to be witnessed these barbaric pageants, as repugnant to political principles as to human feelings, during which insults were poured over misfortune, scorn over ruins and slander upon tombs. Every magnanimous thought, every serviceable truth may be expressed in this assembly. I am doing honor, in the presence of other warriors, to a warrior steadfast in reverses, modest in victory and always human in either fortune. I praise, before the ministers of the French Republic, a man who never yielded to the impulses of ambition and who devoted himself to the needs of his country; a man who, through a destiny wholly uncommon in those who change the faces of empires, died quietly, as a private individual, in his native land, where he had occupied the highest post, after freeing it with his own hands.

What Frenchman, gifted with any power of imagination, does not recall with rapture the moment when Fame published that Freedom was raising her standard among the peoples of America. The old world, bent under the weight of vices and calamities which crushed it in its decaying age, recovered a measure of enthusiasm and turned its eyes towards the distant regions where a new era seemed to be dawning for the human race. At that moment, all prayed for freedom and these prayers were heard even from palaces and kingly thrones. The seas of Europe marvelled to find themselves bearing royal fleets sailing swiftly to the defense of the American republicans.

Oh times of sweetest hope! Oh memories of early youth! With what anxiety we then questioned navigators returning from the ports of Charles-Town and Boston! How we grieved over the reverses of those brave American militias that neither disasters nor weariness or need ever discouraged! How eagerly we rejoiced over the first victories of Washington! Did not Franklin, the wise negotiator who assisted Washington in such a noble cause, receive our homage when he appeared, in Paris and even in Versailles, as an exemplar of the noble simplicity of republican manners? He took his abode upon the banks of this river, opposite the place where we are now gathered. I saw and several among you beheld the venerable aspect of this aged man reminding one of the ancient legislator of the Scythians visiting Athens. Sometimes the negotiator and the hero of the thirteen United States held opposed views; but their wills were ever united when it was necessary to work for the common good of their country. Their names, often joined in common praise during their lives must not be separated after their death. If the spirit of Franklin should return to wander along these banks he enjoyed for so long, it would doubtless applaud the honors we are paying to Washington.

It belongs to the warriors who surround me and to them alone to determine the place that Washington will hold among illustrious military heroes. His successes evidenced more firmness than brilliance, and reason rather than enthusiasm was uppermost in his methods of commanding and fighting. Moreover, the military wonders accomplished by the French armies have overshadowed the fame of all those who had previously gained fame in the same career. Henceforth no people can set models of heroism to a nation exemplifying the whole range of heroism. But Washington offers us other lessons no less worthy of emulation. Amidst the attending disorders of the battlefield, and the inevitable excesses of civil war, humanity took refuge under his tent and was never driven off. Whether triumphant or in adverse circumstances he remained always as calm as wisdom itself and as simple as virtue. Kind feelings always prevailed deep in his heart, even when the interests of his own cause would have justified

131

in a measure the enforcement of the laws of retaliation. I call you to witness, young Asgill, whose misfortune could arouse the interest of England, France and America. What careful sympathy was evidenced by Washington in the postponement of a sentence which the laws of war would have authorized him to execute without delay. He waited until a voice then all powerful was heard clear across the wide ocean asking for a pardon which he could not refuse.* He allowed himself to be moved by that appeal which corresponded to the dictates of his own heart and the day when an innocent victim was spared must be recorded among the most honorable of independent and victorious America.

Let us entertain no doubt on this point: the impulses of a magnanimous spirit bring to a term and uphold revolutions more surely than trophies and victories. The esteem in which the character of the American general was held contributed more than his sword to the independence of his country.

When a tottering government undergoes a violent change, all the neighboring states look upon it with anxiety and fear; reassurance comes only when that state resumes its regular and steady motions. A nation in the throes of a revolution no longer has allies or friends. It invokes in vain former treaties; all the traditional bonds which connected it with the others and held it together are broken; it stands isolated in the midst of a terrified world. People run away from it as one does from a volcano. Following such great political convulsions a man out of the ordinary must manifest himself and through the sole power of his glory check the daring of all factions and restore order from the midst of confusion. He must, if I dare say it, resemble that god of mythology, that sovereign ruler of the winds and the seas, who silenced all the raging storms when he raised his brow above the waves. Only then can the more peaceful governments approach again the nation whose convulsions and aggressions they dreaded.

In fact, it was only when Washington had convinced his enemies that he had sufficient strength to govern peacefully

* That of Queen Marie-Antoinette.

America after such a long upheaval, that peace was concluded under his auspices, that the freedom of the United States was proclaimed from the banks of the Delaware to the banks of the Thames. Thus everything in his history is for us a succession of lessons and hopes.

The characteristics of the American Revolution manifested themselves again not unfrequently during the French Revolution. The Colonies had arisen in rebellion against their mother-country and demanded their independence. Even though this independence had already been acknowledged, the Colonies were not happy. All the factions were still lined up against one another; every petty ambition, every hatred were still seething in men's hearts. So long as a foreign war rages against a country that is changing its form of government, the popular passions are united by a common interest in the defense of the national territory. It is the only time when self-preservation forces upon them the recognition of some authority. Their roars are silenced by the din of battles and the pæans of victory. But with the return of peace, they feel no longer bound by the same fears or the same restraint. Their blind ardor sometimes turns against the very man who saved the threatened country. Washington had foreseen these dangers; but he had the remedies in readiness. He did not believe that the peace he had just concluded would suffice to insure internal security. He had gained the victory over England: against the lawlessness of the many factions, he entered into a fight no less difficult and no less fraught with glory.

However he strove to leave no opening to calumnious accusations. The moment the peace treaty was signed, he resigned in the hands of Congress all the powers with which he had been entrusted. Against his erring fellow citizens he refused to employ anything but the power of persuasion. Had he been a petty schemer, he could have overcome the weakness of the divided factions and having no constitution to restrain his ambition, he could have taken possession of the government whose functions and limits had not yet been determined by any law. Such laws were called for and initiated by Washington himself with an extraordinary perseverance. It was only when it became impossible for ambition to usurp any power that he accepted as the choice of his fellow citizens the honor of governing them for a term of seven years. He had shunned power as long as the use of power could be arbitrary; he was willing to assume this burden only after the exercise of power was restrained within legal bounds. Such a character rightly belongs to the most famous periods of antiquity. As we review the traits which he embodied, we wonder how he could appear in our time. It seems as if we had found again the lost life of one of those illustrious men so admirably depicted by Plutarch.

He administered domestic affairs kindly though firmly, foreign affairs nobly and prudently. He always was respectful of the ways of other nations, just as he demanded respect for the rights of the American people. Thus in all negotiations, the heroic simplicity of the President of the United States could meet the majesty of kings, without boastfulness and without abasement. Let us not look, in his administration for those concepts which our century calls great, and which he would have only considered as reckless. His ideas were marked with more wisdom than audacity: he did not arouse admiration; but he always deserved the same degree of esteem in the field and in the Senate, in the midst of state affairs and in his retreat.

He is one of these living prodigies who from time to time appear upon the world stage with the stamp of grandeur and leadership. Some mysterious and superior cause sends them forth at the proper time, to make a cradle for empires or to restore their ruins. It is in vain that such foreordained men keep aside or hide in the masses: the hand of fortune snatches them up suddenly to bear them swiftly over every obstacle, and from one triumph to another even to the zenith of power. A sort of supernatural inspiration animates all their ideas: all their undertakings receive an irresistible impetus. The crowd still looks for them in their midst and finds them no more; but if they raise their eyes toward loftier regions, they behold in an orb dazzling with light and glory the very man who formerly was looked upon as a heedless adventurer by the ignorant and the envious. Washington lacked the proud and imposing characteristics which impress all minds: he exhibited more orderliness and exactness than vigour and elevation in his plans. He possessed especially to a superior degree, that quality believed to be common, but very rare, that quality no less useful to the government of a nation than to the conduct of life, which sets the mind at rest instead of stirring it and brings more happiness than prestige to those who are endowed with it as well as to those who receive the benefits of its applications: I am speaking of common sense; common sense of which the ancient rules have too often been rejected by pride and which it is high time to restore to all of its rights. Daring destroys, genius elevates, common sense preserves and perfects. To genius has been entrusted the glory of empires; but common sense alone can ensure their peace and duration.

Washington was born in an opulence which he has nobly enhanced amidst agricultural pursuits, as the heroes of ancient Rome. Although he was an enemy of vain ostentation, he wished that republican customs be clad with dignity. None among his fellow countrymen loved liberty more keenly than he; none feared more than he the exaggerated notions of demagogues. His mind, fond of orderliness, constantly avoided every excess: he dared not scorn the teachings of the past; he neither wished to change nor to destroy everything at once; in this regard he held to the doctrine of the legislators of old.

Indeed when these great men had fostered customs and feelings in the minds and souls of their fellow-citizens, they believed their task almost completed: they built systems of morals rather than systems of laws; they had so much respect for the omnipotence of custom that they spared ancient prejudices outwardly incompatible with the new order of things. Greece and Rome when passing from the rule of kings to that of Archons and Consuls were not compelled to change either their various cults or their manners and customs. The

135

first leaders of these republics were no doubt aware that too evident a scorn for the authority and traditions of past ages would weaken morality by debasing old age in the eyes of youth. They were afraid of aiming too hard a blow at the majesty of the past and at attachment for traditions.

I do not wander from my subject in recalling the memory of those founders of ancient republics among whom posterity will rank Washington. As they did, he founded his government on feelings and affection rather than on decrees and laws; he remained, as they did, unassuming at the height of his glory; and as they did, he retained his greatness after withdrawing from public affairs. He had accepted authority only to make secure public prosperity; he would not accept it again when he realized that America was happy and no longer needed his services. He wished to share peacefully, like any ordinary citizen, the happiness this great people had received from him. But it was in vain that he gave up the highest office; the first name in America still remained that of Washington.

Four years had scarcely gone by, since he had left the government. The man, who for a long time commanded armies, was President of thirteen States, lived without ambition in the quiet of the countryside, on a large estate tilled by his own hands amidst the many flocks which had multiplied under his care in the solitudes of a new world. The end of his life was stamped by all the domestic and patriarchal virtues after receiving the lustre of all the military and political virtues. America regarded with reverence the retreat inhabited by its defender; and from this retreat where so much glory was sheltered often issued forth wise counsels which had no less weight than when he was in power. His fellow countrymen could hope to heed his advice for a long time to come, but death suddenly snatched him away from the quietest and most praiseworthy occupations of old age.

Sorrowful wailings were heard from the very heart of America, the land he had freed. It behoved France to be the first to respond to this funereal dirge which must find an echo in all great souls. These majestic walls have been properly designated for the apotheosis of a hero. The shades of Washington, descending upon this lofty dome, will seek here the shades of Turenne, Catinat and the great Condé still finding pleasure in haunting this abode. If these illustrious warriors did not all serve the same cause during their lives, a common fame unites them now that they are no more. Opinions, subject to the caprice of peoples and time, opinions, feeble and vacillating part of our nature, disappear with us in the tomb; but glory and virtue remain forever. Through them great men of all times and from all countries become in some fashion compatriots and contemporaries. They belong to one single family, whose examples are transmitted and renewed from successor to successor. Thus within these martial walls Washington's valor attracts the attention of Condé; his moderation is worthy of Turenne's; his philosophy brings him even closer to Catinat. A people who would accept this ancient and touching dogma of the transmigration of souls would doubtless believe that the soul of Catinat had returned more than once to dwell in the soul of Washington.

But the republican and bellicose strains echoed everywhere by these walls must be especially pleasing to the defender of America. Could he refrain from loving these soldiers who, following his example, repulsed the enemies of their native land? With delight he draws near these veterans whose noble scars are the main ornament of this occasion and some of whom may have fought beside him along the rivers and in the forests of Carolina and Virginia. He rejoices in reviewing these banners wrested from the Asiatic and African barbarians amazed by our boldness.

Their spoils adorn fittingly the funeral of a leader who loved enlightenment and freedom. But there still remains a tribute even more worthy of him: the union of France and America, the happiness of both, the establishment of peace through the new and the old worlds. It seems to me that from the heights of this majestic dome Washington is proclaiming to the whole of France: "Magnanimous nation

137

who knows so well how to honor glory, I won battles in order to secure independence, but the happiness of my country was the reward of this victory. Do not be content to imitate the first half of my life; the second recommends me to the praise of posterity."

Yea, your counsel will be heard, O Washington! O warrior! O legislator! O citizen without reproach! He, who still young surpassed you in battles, following your example will heal with his triumphant hands the wounds of the nation. Soon, his staunch will vouches for it, as well as his military genius if unfortunately it were needed, soon the hymn of peace will be heard in this temple of war; then a universal feeling of joy will wipe out the memory of every injustice and every oppression. Even now the oppressed, forgetting the wrongs they have suffered, confidently look forward to the future. The acclamation of the ages will follow at last the hero who bestows this blessing upon France and upon a world whose foundations she has too long shaken. (*Editor's translation. Fontanes, Œuvres,* vol. II, p. 147-160.)

V.

A Later Generation of Admirers

HYDE DE NEUVILLE
BARBÉ-MARBOIS
TOCQUEVILLE
GUIZOT

Hyde de Neuville

Baron Hyde de Neuville trying to escape from the clutches of Napoleon's police came for the first time to the United States in 1807 and stayed until 1814. The former exile came back as Minister plenipotentiary from the French court in 1816-1820; and visited the country for a last time in 1821-1822. His *Mémoires et souvenirs* were published in Paris, 2 vols., 1888-1892 and translated into English with a more descriptive and picturesque title: *Memoirs of Baron Hyde de Neuville; Outlaw, Exile, Ambassador*. London, 1913. The staunch royalist opinions of the ambassador of Louis XVIII did not lessen in any way his admiration for George Washington. If he made some reservations in his forecast of the future of the United States, he could not entirely avoid the "contagious" influence of American liberalism and praised in the highest manner the civic virtues of the American founders.

WASHINGTON TYPIFIES AMERICA

I may be mistaken, but on observing America at close range one has the feeling of something still unknown stirring in the future; one feels that the tyrannical power which oppresses our unfortunate country is not the last word of the century which has just begun and that a new wind is blowing over the world, at the same time a cause and a result of our own revolution. Its influence cannot remain localized, and it is probable that it will bring about some modifications in all the societies to come. Its ultimate consequences cannot be easily foreseen and will develop but slowly; yet, at times, one would like to hold to the belief that America has guessed the riddle of the future and advanced ahead of our own times.

She has nothing in common with the ancient republics. They worshipped the grandeur of the fatherland; Americans have only need and consciousness of its prosperity. They ambition a glory more moderate, more modest, more durable which would cast little glamor through the annals of history but as time goes on will demonstrate its strength.

The national hero of America typifies excellently the country which gave him birth. My judgment of Washington is based much more upon what he has left behind him than on what he did during his lifetime; great men should be measured by what survives of their works; but in that case how few would remain standing on the pedestal which they have built for themselves among their contemporaries. The majority of men whose names once was heard throughout the world have destroyed rather than they have built. Most of the time, it is the sword that carves a place in history, and posterity, imbued with the prejudice that confuses glamour and glory, most often pays tribute to the memories of the men who were the dazzling scourges of their times.

The great figure of Washington will stand out among this mass of great men with a glory purer although less resounding. He was truly the benefactor of his country; he drew his line of conduct from its needs and its age-old feelings while making no concession to his personal pride. He did not seek abroad for personal triumphs; he did not strive to aggrandize his beloved country, but he wished to establish it strongly, and after making it truly free, he stopped, thus setting an example of this moderation in which resides the real strength of governments and should be the supreme glory of heroes. (*Editor's translation*. Hyde de Neuville, vol. I, p. 467, 468, 469.)

Barbé-Marbois

As a young diplomat, secretary to M. de la Luzerne, Barbé-Marbois had paid his respects to Washington (see p. 74). When late in life he wrote his classic *Histoire de la Louisiane,*

Paris, 1829, in which he related the negotiations in which he had participated so effectively, his early enthusiasm had not weakened. The sober, mature and well considered judgment of a man who had served Louis XVI, the Republic, Napoleon and Louis XVIII, or rather had done his work and his duty to his country under different regimes, cannot easily be dismissed and sums up the views of several generations of French admirers of Washington.

"GREATER THAN ALEXANDER OR CÆSAR"

A most illuminating justification of the American Revolution and of the assistance given by France can be found in the advantages which have accrued from it to society in general and even to England herself. It belongs to the American people to establish their Revolution even more securely through the moderation of their conduct.

Among the civilians chosen as leaders by these new peoples after the declaration of their independence, among those to whom they entrusted the command of their armies, only one, Arnold, was misled by ambition and avarice; no one else took advantage of public misfortunes in order to gain advancement or to increase one's wealth. One witnessed a development devoid of display and ostentation of the virtues necessary to the foundation and preservation of States, courage in new undertakings, moderation in successes, steadfastness in reverses. These leaders received their fair share of the fame which is won on battlefields, is accompanied with a larger amount of danger and for this reason is placed above all others by the public.

Washington, remains greater in the eyes of his fellow citizens than Alexander or Cæsar ever were for the Greeks and the Romans. His natural moderation was such, that after defeating the enemies of his country, unlike so many men who have acquired military glory, he had not to overcome his own ambition. He was satisfied to put away his sword in order to devote himself to the government of a republic

143

at last at peace. Desolation and ruins are the monuments which commemorate the careers of conquerors and mark their passage on this earth. Men's happiness, such is the unperishable monument that will remind future generations of the name of Washington. His glory is purer than the conqueror's; in fact it is greater than the fame of the so-called sons of the gods. When the war was over, the American people took to heart to pay a special tribute to his civic virtues.

To-day they prize one particular glory above all others: the glory which in peace times is bound to a sincere love of the country, which grows from a modest desire of obtaining the esteem of one's fellow citizens, but is devoid of ambitious passions and is almost indifferent to fame. (*Editor's translation.* Barbé-Marbois, p. 16, 17, 18.)

Tocqueville

Tocqueville seldom mentioned Washington in his great book. In fact, he discussed institutions and not men and was not much interested in history and origins. On one particular occasion, however, when discussing the principles on which rest the foreign policies of the United States, he departed from this reserve and gave full credit to Washington for formulating the fundamental rules which ought to direct the conduct of the President and the Senate in dealing with foreign nations. Even after a century has elapsed his opinion is well worth examining. The translation of Henry Reeve, often reprinted, has been used here, from the edition published in 1904 by Appleton, New York.

WASHINGTON AND AMERICA'S FOREIGN POLICY

We have seen that the Federal Constitution intrusts the permanent direction of the external interests of the nation to the President and the Senate, which tends in some degree to detach the general foreign policy of the Union from the control of the people. It can not therefore be asserted with truth that the external affairs of State are conducted by the democracy.

The policy of America owes its rise to Washington, and after him to Jefferson, who established those principles which it observes at the present day. Washington said in the admirable letter which he addressed to his fellow-citizens, and which may be looked upon as his political ,bequest to the country: "The great rule of conduct for us in regard to foreign nations is, in extending our commercial relations, to have with them as little political connection as possible. So far as we have already formed engagements, let them be fulfilled with perfect good faith. Here let us stop. Europe has a set of primary interests which to us have none, or a very remote relation. Hence, she must be engaged in frequent controversies, the causes of which are essentially foreign to our concerns. Hence, therefore, it must be unwise in us to implicate ourselves, by artificial ties, in the ordinary vicissitudes of her politics, or the ordinary combinations and collisions of her friendships or enmities. Our detached and distant situation invites and enables us to pursue a different course. If we remain one people, under an efficient government, the period is not far off when we may defy material injury from external annoyance; when we may take such an attitude as will cause the neutrality we may at any time resolve upon to be scrupulously respected; when belligerent nations, under the impossibility of making acquisitions upon us, will not lightly hazard the giving us provocation; when we may choose peace or war, as our interest, guided by justice, shall counsel. Why forego the advantages of so peculiar a situation? Why quit our own to stand upon foreign ground? Why, by interweaving our destiny with that of any part of Europe, entangle our peace and prosperity in the toils of European ambition, rivalship, interest, humour, or caprice? It is our true policy to steer clear of permanent alliances with any portion of the foreign world; so far, I mean, as we are now at liberty to do it; for let me not be understood as capable of patronizing infidelity to existing engagements. I hold the maxim no less applicable

145

to public than to private affairs, that honesty is always the best policy. I repeat it, therefore, let those engagements be observed in their genuine sense; but in my opinion it is unnecessary, and would be unwise, to extend them. Taking care always to keep ourselves, by suitable establishments, in a respectable defensive posture, we may safely trust to temporary alliances for extraordinary emergencies." In a previous part of the same letter Washington makes the following admirable and just remark: "The nation which indulges toward another an habitual hatred or an habitual fondness is in some degree a slave. It is a slave to its animosity or to its affection, either of which is sufficient to lead it astray from its duty and its interest."

The political conduct of Washington was always guided by these maxims. He succeeded in maintaining his country in a state of peace while all the other nations of the globe were at war; and he laid it down as a fundamental doctrine, that the true interest of the Americans consisted in a perfect neutrality with regard to the internal dissensions of the European Powers.

Jefferson went still further, and introduced a maxim into the policy of the Union which affirms that "the Americans ought never to solicit any privileges from foreign nations, in order not to be obliged to grant similar privileges themselves."

These two principles, which were so plain and so just as to be adapted to the capacity of the populace, have greatly simplified the foreign policy of the United States. As the Union takes no part in the affairs of Europe, it has, properly speaking, no foreign interests to discuss, since it has at present no powerful neighbours on the American continent. The country is as much removed from the passions of the Old World by its position as by the line of policy which it has chosen, and it is neither called upon to repudiate nor to espouse the conflicting interests of Europe; while the dissensions of the New World are still concealed within the bosom of the future.

The Union is free from all pre-existing obligations, and it is consequently enabled to profit by the experience of the old nations of Europe, without being obliged, as they are, to make the best of the past, and to adapt it to their present circumstances; or to accept that immense inheritance which they derive from their forefathers—an inheritance of glory mingled with calamities, and of alliances conflicting with national antipathies. The foreign policy of the United States is reduced by its very nature to await the chances of the future history of the nation, and for the present it consists more in abstaining from interference than in exerting its activity.

It is therefore very difficult to ascertain at present what degree of sagacity the American democracy will display in the conduct of the foreign policy of the country; and upon this point its adversaries, as well as its advocates, must suspend their judgment. As for myself, I have no hesitation in avowing my conviction that it is most especially in the conduct of foreign relations that democratic governments appear to me to be decidedly inferior to governments carried on upon different principles. Experience, instruction, and habit may almost always succeed in creating a species of practical discretion in democracies, and that science of the daily occurrences of life which is called good sense. Good sense may suffice to direct the ordinary course of society; and among a people whose education has been provided for, the advantages of democratic liberty in the internal affairs of the country may more than compensate for the evils inherent in a democratic government. But such is not always the case in the mutual relations of foreign nations.

Foreign politics demand scarcely any of those qualities which a democracy possesses; and they require, on the contrary, the perfect use of almost all those faculties in which it is deficient. Democracy is favourable to the increase of the internal resources of the State; it tends to diffuse a moderate independence; it promotes the growth of public spirit, and fortifies the respect which is entertained for law in all classes of society; and these are advantages which only exercise an indirect influence over the relations which one people bears to another. But a democracy is unable to regulate the details of an important undertaking, to persevere in a design, and to work out its execution in the presence of serious obstacles. It can not combine its measures with secrecy, and it will not await their consequences with patience. These are qualities which more especially belong to an individual or to an aristocracy; and they are precisely the means by which an individual people attains to a predominant position.

If, on the contrary, we observe the natural defects of aristocracy, we shall find that their influence is comparatively innoxious in the direction of the external affairs of a State. The capital fault of which aristocratic bodies may be accused is that they are more apt to contrive their own advantage than that of the mass of the people. In foreign politics it is rare for the interest of the aristocracy to be in any way distinct from that of the people.

The propensity which democracies have to obey the impulse of passion rather than the suggestions of prudence, and to abandon a mature design for the gratification of a momentary caprice, was very clearly seen in America on the breaking out of the French Revolution. It was then as evident to the simplest capacity as it is at the present time that the interest of the Americans forbade them to take any part in the contest which was about to deluge Europe with blood, but which could by no means injure the welfare of their own country. Nevertheless, the sympathies of the people declared themselves with so much violence in behalf of France that nothing but the inflexible character of Washington, and the immense popularity which he enjoyed, could have prevented the Americans from declaring war against England. And even then, the exertions which the austere reason of that great man made to repress the generous but imprudent passions of his fellow-citizens, very nearly deprived him of the sole recompense which he had ever claimed—that of his country's love. The majority then reprobated the line of policy which he adopted, and which has since been unanimously approved by the nation. If the Constitution and the favour of the public had not intrusted the direction of the foreign affairs of the country to Washington, it is certain that the American nation would at that time have taken the very measures which it now condemns.

Almost all the nations which have ever exercised a powerful influence upon the destinies of the world by conceiving, following up, and executing vast designs—from the Romans to the English—have been governed by aristocratic institutions. Nor will this be a subject of wonder when we recollect that nothing in the world has so absolute a fixity of purpose as an aristocracy. The mass of the people may be led astray by ignorance or passion; the mind of a king may be biassed, and his perseverance in his designs may be shaken—besides which a king is not immortal. But an aristocratic body is too numerous to be led astray by the blandishments of intrigue, and yet not numerous enough to yield readily to the intoxicating influence of unreflecting passion: it has the energy of a firm and enlightened individual, added to the power which it derives from its perpetuity.

Guizot

Written in 1839 as an introduction to the French translation of Sparks's *Life of Washington,* Guizot's essay was printed in English, in Boston, in 1840. In spite of its grandiose style it expresses well the views of the many French students of American affairs who believed the French people could not borrow American institutions and follow closely the American constitution, but to whom Washington remained the greatest leader of modern times and an example for the rulers of the old world.

THE MOST FORTUNATE OF ALL GREAT MEN

Washington did well to withdraw from public business. He had entered upon it at one of those moments, at once difficult and favorable, when nations, surrounded by perils, summon all their virtue and all their wisdom to surmount them. He was admirably suited to his position. He held the sentiments and opinions of his age without slavishness or fanaticism. The past, its institutions, its interests, its manners, inspired him with neither hatred nor regret. His thoughts and his ambition did not impatiently reach forward into the future. The society, in the midst of which he lived, suited his tastes and his judgment. He had confidence in its principles and its destiny; but a confidence enlightened and qualified by an accurate instinctive perception of the eternal principles of social order. He served it with heartiness and independence, with that combination of faith and fear which is wisdom in the affairs of the world, as well as before God. On this account, especially, he was qualified to govern it; for democracy requires two things for its tranquillity and its success; it must feel itself to be trusted and yet restrained, and must believe alike in the genuine devotedness and the moral superiority of its leaders. On these conditions alone can it govern itself while in a process of development, and hope to take place among the durable and glorious forms of human society. It is the honor of the American people to have, at this period, understood and accepted these conditions. It is the glory of Washington to have been their interpreter and instrument.

He did the two greatest things which, in politics, man can have the privilege of attempting. He maintained, by peace, that independence of his country, which he had acquired by war. He founded a free government, in the name of the principles of order, and by reëstablishing their sway.

When he retired from public life, both tasks were accomplished, and he could enjoy the result. For, in such high enterprises, the labor which they have cost matters but little. The sweat of any toil is dried at once on the brow where God places such laurels.

He retired voluntarily, and a conqueror. To the very last, his policy had prevailed. If he had wished, he could still have kept the direction of it. His successor was one of his most attached friends, one whom he had himself designated.

Still the epoch was a critical one. He had governed successfully for eight years, a long period in a democratic state, and that in its infancy. For some time, a policy opposed to his own had been gaining ground. American society seemed disposed to make a trial of new paths, more in conformity, perhaps, with its bias. Perhaps the hour had come for Washington to quit the arena. His successor was then overcome. Mr. Adams was succeeded by Mr. Jefferson, the leader of the opposition. Since that time, the democratic party has governed the United States.

Is it a good or an evil? Could it be otherwise? Had the government continued in the hands of the federal party, would it have done better? Was this possible? What have been the consequences, to the United States, of the triumph of the democratic party? Have they carried out to the end, or have they only begun? What changes have the society and constitution of America undergone, what have they yet to undergo, under their influence?

These are great questions; difficult, if I mistake not, for natives to solve, and certainly impossible for a foreigner.

However it may be, one thing is certain; that which Washington did,—the founding of a free government, by order and peace, at the close of the Revolution,—no other policy than his could have accomplished. He has had this true glory; of triumphing, so long as he governed; and of rendering the triumph of his adversaries possible, after him, without disturbance to the state.

More than once, perhaps, this result presented itself to his mind, without disturbing his composure. "With me, a predominant motive has been to endeavour to gain time to our country to settle and mature its recent institutions; and to progress without interruption to that degree of strength and consistency, which is necessary to give it, humanly speaking the command of its own fortunes."*

* Washington's Writings, Vol. XII. p. 234.

The people of the United States are virtually the arbiters of their own fortunes. Washington had aimed at that high object. He reached his mark.

Who has succeeded like him? Who has seen his own success so near and so soon? Who has enjoyed, to such a degree, and to the last, the confidence and gratitude of his country?

Still, at the close of his life, in the delightful and honorable retirement at Mount Vernon, which he had so longed for, this great man, serene as he was, was inwardly conscious of a slight feeling of lassitude and melancholy; a feeling very natural at the close of a long life employed in the affairs of men. Power is an oppressive burden; and mankind are hard to serve, when one is struggling virtuously against their passions and their errors. Even success does not efface the sad impressions which the contest has given birth to; and the exhaustion, which succeeds the struggle, is still felt in the quiet of repose.

The disposition of the most eminent men, and of the best among the most eminent, to keep aloof from public affairs, in a free democratic society, is a serious fact. Washington, Jefferson, Madison, all ardently sighed for retirement. It would seem as if, in this form of society, the task of government were too severe for men who are capable of comprehending its extent, and desirous of discharging the trust in a proper manner.

Still, to such men alone this task is suited, and ought to be intrusted. Government will be, always and everywhere, the greatest exercise of the faculties of man, and consequently that which requires minds of the highest order. It is for the honor, as well as for the interest of society, that such minds should be drawn into the administration of its affairs, and retained there; for no institutions, no securities, can supply their place.

And, on the other hand, in men who are worthy of this destiny, all weariness, all sadness of spirit, however it might be permitted in others, is a weakness. Their vocation is labor. Their reward is, indeed, the success of their efforts, but still only in labor. Very often they die, bent under the burden, before the day of recompense arrives. Washington lived to receive it. He deserved and enjoyed both success and repose. Of all great men, he was the most virtuous and the most fortunate. In this world, God has no higher favors to bestow. (Guizot, p. 181-188.)

Index

Index

157

Stuart, Mrs., 13
Sullivan, John, 28
Sully, 114
Sutter, 12

Talleyrand, his report to Bonaparte, 125, 127
Talon, Omer, 105
Tarleton, Colonel Bonastre, 49
Ternant, Jean de, xvii, 90; at Mount Vernon, 92-3
Thomas, Antoine-Léonard, 30
Tilghman, Tench, 14, 44, 60
Tocqueville, Alexis de, ix, xv, 114-49
Trenton, battle of, ix, 55, 79n
Turenne, 24, 56, 79n, 137
Turner, Frederick J., 90

Valley Forge, xvii, 13-16, 26
Vasington, tragedy, xi, xii
Vergennes, Comte de, 73
Verplanks Point, camp at, 50 and n
Vioménil, Baron de, 48n
Voltaire, apotheosis of, xi

Walker, Benjamin, 17, 19, 61
Washington, George, his biographers, vii; placed among the heroes by Bonaparte, ix; his military genius, x; loved by the people, xvi; at Mount Vernon, xvii; and the Conway Cabal, 3-9; letter to Lafayette, 8; letter to Lafayette, his melancholy, 10; his staff described by Duponceau, 13; his humor, 18; his tactics, 19; at Valley Forge, 27; his staff, 28; and Jumonville, 29, 30; at Fort Necessity, 29; portrait by Ségur, 36; at West Point, 36; his career by Ségur, 38; at West Point, 40; crosses the Hudson, 42; rejoices like a child, 43; judged by Chastellux, 44; his staff described by Chastellux, 44; described by translator of Chastellux, 44, 45n; his after dinner conversation, 49;

orders wine for Chastellux's translator, 50; his portrait by Chastellux, 55-7; compared with Cæsar, Trajan, Alexander, 55; his noble features, 56; an intimate portrait, 59; his readings on tactics, 59; his headquarters at Newburgh, 61; his portrait by Fersen, 63; dines with C. Blanchard, 64; his table, 65; his grave manners, 65; says grace, 66; love of the people for, 69; his portrait by Robin, 68-9; his lack of ambition, 73; the citizen, 73; meets La Luzerne at Fishkill, 74-6; his simple uniform, 75; his "restricted gaiety," 75; plays ball, 75; abhors swearing, 75; takes the helm, 76; statue ordered by Congress, 79n; inscription for his statue, 79n; his portrait in Mandrillon, 80; refuses tokens of gratitude, 83; masters his pride, 84; at Mount Vernon, 86; as a realist, 88; as a farmer, 87; advocates inoculation, 87; his foreign policies, 90; outplays Ternant, 91; treasures the Bastille's key, 95; opens session of Congress, 99; compared with Aratus, 101-4; unity of his character, 101; criticized by Adet, 106-9; criticized by Genet, 105; judged by Samuel Adams, 107; accused of ambition, 108; his statue by Houdon, 110; retires from public life, 111-13; tribute by Crèvecœur, 117-18; drinks "cyder," 118; his portrait by a French artist, 119; at tea, 120; his views on American manufactures, 120; admiration of Bonaparte for, 127-9; his eulogy by Fontanes, 129-38; characterized by Hyde de Neuville, 141; typifies America, 141; homage of Barbé-Marbois, 142-4; the builder of a nation, 144; his foreign policies defended by